Chatter

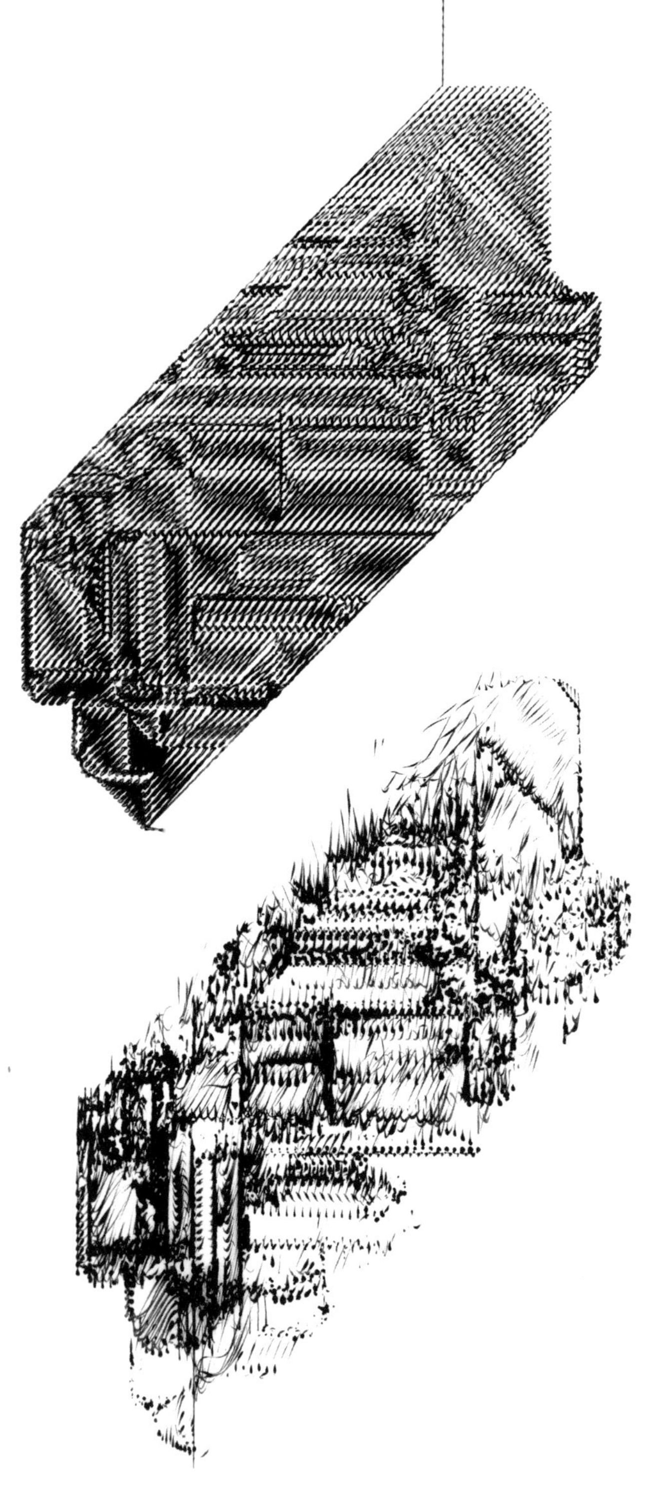

Chatter

Architecture Talks Back

Karen Kice

The Art Institute of Chicago
Distributed by Yale University Press, New Haven and London

A+D SERIES

A+D SERIES

Chatter: Architecture Talks Back was published in conjunction with an exhibition of the same title organized by and presented at the Art Institute of Chicago from April 11 to July 12, 2015.

Support for the exhibition and the catalogue is provided by John H. and Neville Bryan, Celia and David Hilliard, the Butler-VanderLinden Family Fund for Architecture and Design, the Architecture and Design Committee Fund, and the Architecture & Design Society.

First edition
Printed in the United States of America

ISBN: 978-0-300-21063-7

Published by
The Art Institute of Chicago
111 South Michigan Avenue
Chicago, Illinois 60603-6404
www.artic.edu

Distributed by
Yale University Press
302 Temple Street
P.O. Box 209040
New Haven, Connecticut 06520-9040
www.yalebooks.com/art

Produced by the Department of Publishing at the Art Institute of Chicago, Sarah Guernsey, Executive Director
Edited by Michelle Piranio and Christine Schwab
Production by Joseph Mohan and Lauren Makholm
Photography research by Katie Levi
Unless otherwise noted, photography of works of art is by Christopher Gallagher and Robert Lifson, with postproduction by Jonathan Mathias, Department of Imaging, the Art Institute of Chicago.
Series design by 2 × 4, New York
Design and typesetting by Jeff Wonderland, Director, Department of Graphic Design, the Art Institute of Chicago
Separations, printing, and binding by Classic Color, Broadview, Illinois

Library of Congress Cataloging-in-Publication Data

Kice, Karen.
Chatter : architecture talks back / Karen Kice. — First edition.
pages cm. — (A+D series)
"Chatter: Architecture Talks Back was published in conjunction with an exhibition of the same title organized by and presented at the Art Institute of Chicago from April 11 to July 12, 2015."
Includes bibliographical references.
ISBN 978-0-300-21063-7 (paperback)
1. Architecture, Modern—21st century—Exhibitions. 2. Communication in architectural design—Exhibitions. I. Art Institute of Chicago. II. Title.
NA687.K53 2015
724'.7—dc23
2014049263

Cover: Bureau Spectacular / Jimenez Lai, assisted by Senaid Selcin and Frank Gossage, *Cartoonish Metropolis*, 2011

Page 2: Erin Besler, Low Fidelity, robot-drawn elevations of foam object-projections of the white space of Peter Eisenman's thirteenth House VI transformation, at speeds of 1 (top) and 100 (bottom) percent, 2012

Page 6: John Szot, Architecture and the Unspeakable, conceptual collage, 2014

Pages 10–11: Luis Urculo for Fake Industries Architectural Agonism with MAIO, Rooms: No Vacancy, video still frame, 2014

Previous books in the A+D Series
Douglas Garofalo (2006)
Young Chicago (2006)
Figuration in Contemporary Design (2007)
Graphic Thought Facility (2008)
Konstantin Grcic (2009)
Fashioning the Object (2012)

This book was made using paper and materials certified by the Forest Stewardship Council®, which ensures responsible forest management.

Contents

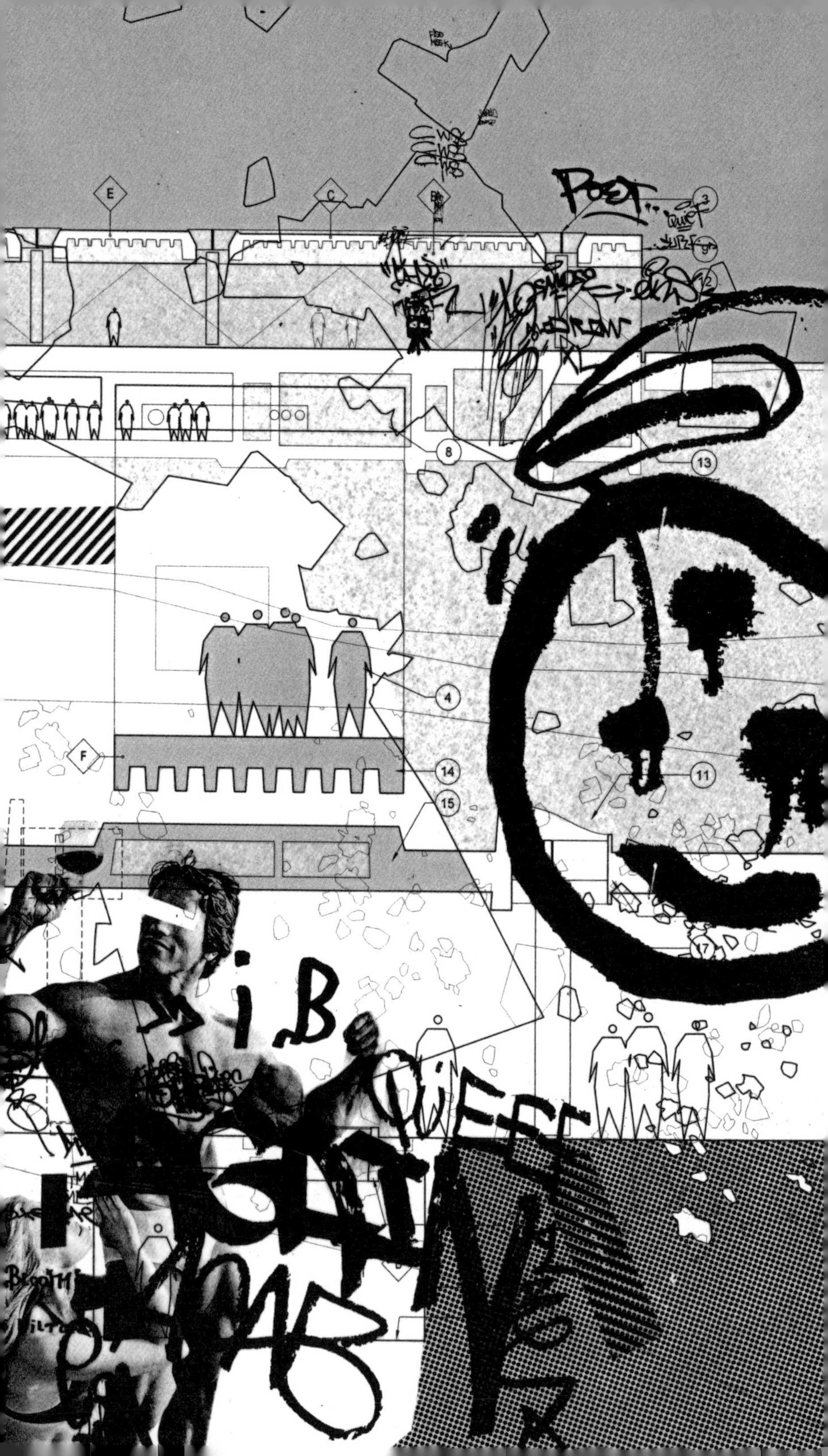

Support for the exhibition and the catalogue is provided by John H. and Neville Bryan, Celia and David Hilliard, the Butler-VanderLinden Family Fund for Architecture and Design, the Architecture and Design Committee Fund, and the Architecture & Design Society.

Foreword

Chatter: Architecture Talks Back is the seventh installment of the Art Institute of Chicago's A+D Series. Organized by Karen Kice, Neville Bryan Assistant Curator of Architecture and Design, the exhibition and catalogue are devoted to five contemporary architectural practices—Bureau Spectacular, Formlessfinder, Fake Industries Architectural Agonism, Erin Besler, and John Szot Studio—and the diverse methods and approaches that drive their work. Kice explores these practitioners' efforts to examine and expand the meanings of architecture, looking not only at how new modes of communication have influenced the ways in which they construct and present their ideas and projects, but also at the role that the history of the discipline continues to play in their work.

On behalf of the museum and the Department of Architecture and Design, I express our sincere gratitude to the Architecture & Design Society for their continued support over the years. The exhibition and the catalogue are also made possible through the generosity of John H. and Neville Bryan, Celia and David Hilliard, the Butler-VanderLinden Family Fund for Architecture and Design, and the Architecture and Design Committee Fund.

We are deeply grateful to the featured architects and designers for their contributions and dedication to this project: Jimenez Lai of Bureau Spectacular; Garrett Ricciardi and Julian Rose of Formlessfinder; Cristina Goberna and Urtzi Grau of Fake Industries Architectural Agonism; Erin Besler; and John Szot.

Special thanks go to the members of the Department of Architecture and Design, especially Zoë Ryan, John H. Bryan Chair and Curator, along with Alison Fisher, Lori Boyer, Daniel Dorough, Alicja Zelazko, Jennifer Breckner, Gibran Villalobos, and interns Corinna Anderson and Kevin Schmidt.

The Departments of Exhibitions and Museum Registration, led by Jennifer Draffen—in particular Jennifer Paoletti, Megan Rader, Sally-Ann Felgenhauer, Jennifer Oberhauser, and Allison Revello—expertly managed the safe transport of artworks for the exhibition. The Art Institute's legal staff, especially Julie Getzels, Maria Simon, and Troy Klyber, provided key assistance. We also owe many thanks to the Department of Museum Development, including Eve Coffee Jeffers, James Allan, Jennifer Moran, and George Martin.

We recognize the outstanding work of the Department of Publishing under Sarah Guernsey, including Joseph Mohan, Christine Schwab, Lauren Makholm, Wilson McBee, and Katie Levi, along with freelance editor Michelle Piranio. We acknowledge the contributions of museum conservators Antoinette Owen, Kimberly Nichols, Kristi Dahm, Suzanne Schnepp, Emily Heye, and Christine Fabian. Thanks to Jeff Wonderland and his team in the Department of Graphic Design for artful work on the catalogue design and for creating the exhibition graphics. In the Department of Imaging, we thank Christopher Gallagher, Robert Hashimoto, Robert Lifson, Jonathan Mathias, and Amy Zavaleta. We express our appreciation to Sara Urizar, Junia-Elli Jorgji, and Jorge Tobias in the Department of Design and Construction for their expertise in realizing the installation. John Molini, Michael Kaysen, Craig Cox, and the shipping and installation staff handled the works of art with great care. We are grateful to William Caddick and to Tom Ryan, Joseph Vatinno, George Yovkovich, Thomas Panka, Anthony Nakvosas, and their respective staffs in the Department of Physical Plant for their exceptional workmanship. Thanks are also due to Ray Carlson, Jr., William Foster, Thomas Riley, Margaret Skimina, and Salvatore Seminara.

Head of Interpretation and Communication Erin Hogan and, in the Department of Museum Education, Judith Kirshner, Fawn Ring, and Allison Muscolino were invaluable in presenting this exhibition to the public. In the Department of Marketing, special appreciation goes to Gordon Montgomery, Rebecca Baldwin, Nora Gainer, Amanda Hicks, Paul Jones, Lauren Schultz, and Robert Sexton. We acknowledge the fine work of Russell Collett and the Department of Protection Services. Finally, we extend sincere thanks to David Thurm, Chief Operating Officer; Martha Tedeschi, Deputy Director for Art and Research; Jeanne Ladd, Vice President for Museum Finance; and Dawn Koster, Coordinator of Museum Fiscal Affairs.

Douglas Druick
President and Eloise W. Martin Director
The Art Institute of Chicago

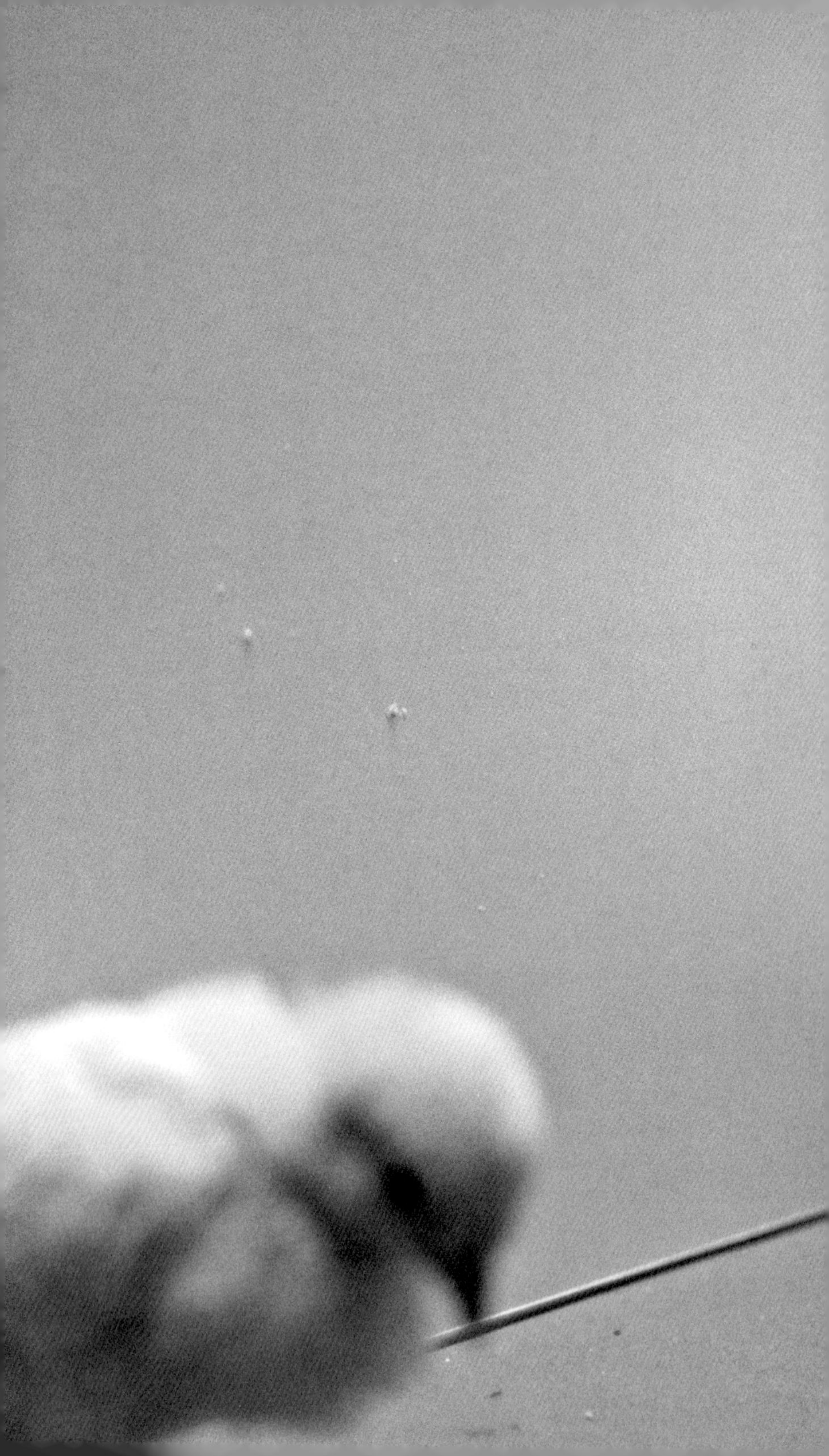

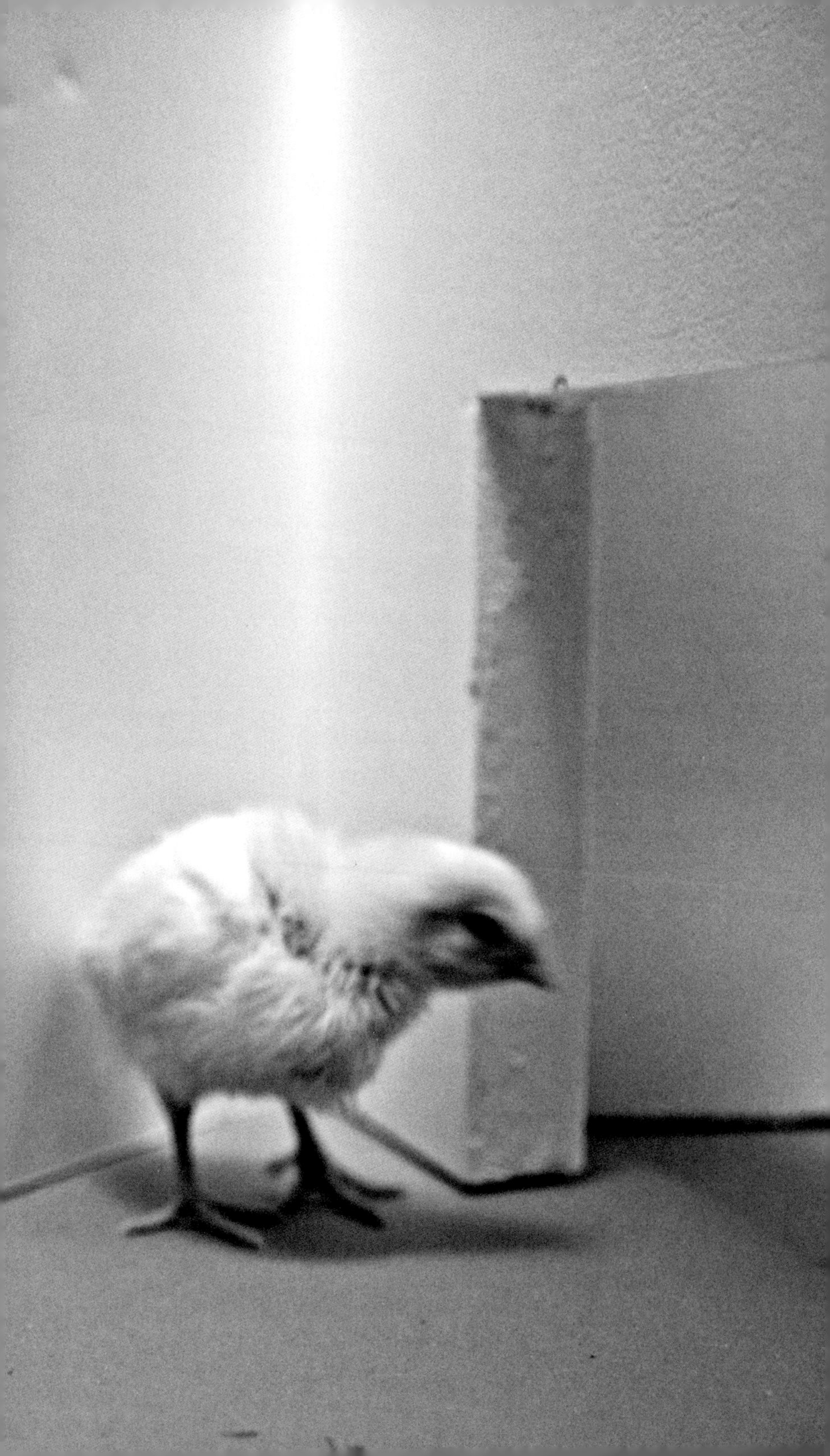

Chatter: Architecture Talks Back

Karen Kice

Over the past decade, a new breed of architects has emerged, characterized by an innate understanding of and adaptability to technology coupled with a heightened sense of history. As continuous and growing flows of information and new technologies have come to define contemporary society, the access to information and the expansion and evolution of modes of communication have had a direct impact on the way architects think about and synthesize concepts for presenting their work. Ideas are easier to disseminate, thanks to a range of outlets and the explosion of print and online publications, as well as wiki applications and Web sites such as Facebook, Instagram, and Twitter. Such platforms allow for instantaneous editing, exchange, and broadcast of information as quickly digestible fragments: a headline, an image, 140 characters. Technology also brings a broader context: architects operate in a globalized environment in which worldwide access to information results in more complex and far-reaching cross-cultural conversations. They are no longer as rooted to the locations in which they work, and many are exporting ideas and projects from one country to another. In architecture, no single style now dominates; rather, the works reflect a compelling pluralism.[1]

The influence of technology is also apparent in the work of these contemporary architects, which is often produced with digital tools to create renderings, video animations, 3-D printed models, and virtual models; such tools have both transformed and expanded the range of representation and production. Yet even as they innovate, these architects demonstrate a strong awareness of and active engagement with the history of the field, many responding overtly to preceding practitioners and projects. Some take a critical stance on the evolution of architecture and its position in culture, anchoring their work in the historical and social narratives embedded within the field, while others question the increased reliance on digital tools. Many combine bits of information into a compilation of ideas, tying in past theories, projects, and narratives. In a crisscrossing of concepts, influences, styles, and cultures, multiple exchanges arise through projects that advance a rethinking of the discipline of architecture. *Chatter: Architecture Talks Back* centers on five emerging practices—Bureau Spectacular, Formlessfinder, Fake Industries Architectural Agonism, Erin Besler, and John Szot Studio—that exemplify these diverse approaches.

Chatter: Theory and Practice

Chatter. The word connotes conversations and narratives formulated and reconstructed from fragmented pieces of information and ideas that are neither comprehensive nor fully comprehensible on their own. While such interchanges might be directed, they do not necessarily coalesce into a continuous flow or direct exchange; rather, they congeal into new multidirectional discussions. This notion reflects how ideas are conveyed in contemporary modes of expression, from texting and tweeting to social media outlets and wiki platforms. Chatter can be linked to current practices in architecture, both in the way it feeds concepts and theories by pulling together bits of information from a variety of resources and in the way ideas and meaning are constructed—as fragmented, multifarious, and open. These various directions can be attributed to a culture of instantaneous sharing, editing, hashtagging, and reposting that creates a need to synthesize and parse data in a coherent manner. Although the term *chatter* might imply insignificant rumblings, it is used here to designate the way information amasses today.[2]

Chatter focuses on a generation of architects that embraces the latest technologies by using contemporary means of production and modes of communication, as well as a range of representational methods and formats—from drawings made by hand or enabled by robots, to graphic novels, to digital simulations. The practitioners featured here also talk back to history, whether by appropriating ideas and styles or by calling attention to overlooked aspects of society. Conceptually, they refer to various aspects of the discipline, offering a mash-up of architectural history and theory; a commentary on the fetishization of form; an investigation of appropriation and the reframing of architecture as an analytical practice; a critical look at the generative capabilities of technology in representation and serial production; and an exploration outside the field to seek inspiration from neglected social contexts.

The activities of rehashing, repackaging, and instantaneously exchanging ideas are not unfamiliar to the field of architecture. They do not derive from a paucity of concepts and theories, but indicate a practice of astute selection and collaboration. In pedagogical formats such as group critiques and through client meetings, work is constantly presented, discussed, and reworked collaboratively. Furthermore, this method of creation often involves a narrative impulse that helps practitioners rationalize and concretize fragmented ideas in new and meaningful ways. As philosopher Richard Kearney asserted, "In our postmodern era of fragmentation and fracture . . . narrative provides us with one of our most viable forms of *identity*—individual and communal."[3] Narrative in architecture is frequently used to give coherence to complex ideas, and it varies greatly in the form it takes, from drawings and diagrams to digital renderings and videos. Though not textual, or necessarily following the sequential structure of narrative in literature, "the conventions are, in a sense," as architectural historian James Ackerman put forth, "elements of a language."[4] The language of architecture—through the use of representations—can be conveyed in a variety of formats, including those that are nonlinear or highly nuanced. For the architects discussed here, the diverse methods they use to present their conversations and embed their narratives are combined with an insightful understanding of digital technologies and tools for the purpose of looking intently at architecture's history. By building on the past, they are developing dialogues, with both those who came before and those around them now. With the multitude of platforms for the exchange of ideas that have emerged over the past two decades, they are able to connect and converse with an immediate, yet global, architecture community. Many of these practitioners are producing blogs, publishing critical writings, or presenting their work via social media to test a variety of theories. Indeed, the trend in presenting work is itself no longer focused on discrete, iconic buildings or complete narratives; instead, the approach is more open-ended—a conversation starter.

Architecture has always had a close relationship to history, using it as a crucial element of production. This notion is similar to the blank page that theorist Sylvia Lavin described: "Full of the densest emptiness, yet equally full of the memory of all things made in the past, the conceptual void embodied by this piece of paper is every maker's greatest challenge. Part of the challenge stems from trying to understand how the nearly intangible thinness of white paper can contain the enormity of all creative space."[5] This relationship to history, however, has varied over time. In the early twentieth century, modern architecture effected a formal shift from previous movements, stripping away elements such as ornamentation and style and establishing a new focus on the concept that form follows function—often read as a divergence from history.[6] In their seminal work *Learning from Las Vegas*, first published in 1972, architects Robert Venturi, Denise Scott Brown, and Steven Izenour unpacked the modern movement to highlight its trajectory: "The architecture of the Modern movement, during its early decades and through a number of its masters, developed a vocabulary of forms based on a variety of industrial models whose conventions and proportions were no less explicit than the Classical orders of the Renaissance. . . . [T]he Moderns employed a design method based on typological models and developed an architectural iconography based on their interpretation of the progressive technology of the Industrial Revolution."[7] The postmodern movement, which emerged as a direct reaction to modernism, reintroduced history by incorporating ideas from the field of semiotics, the philosophical study of the function of signs and symbols in the creation of meaning. Projects such as Venturi and Scott Brown's 1991 Sainsbury Wing for the National Gallery in London (fig. 1) and Chicago-based architect Stanley Tigerman's 1982 Bloch Residence in Highland Park, Illinois (fig. 2), exemplify this direction. In the Sainsbury Wing, Venturi and Scott Brown added columns that did not function as supports but were embedded in the facade as references to the history of the site and to visually connect the new wing to William Wilkins's adjacent

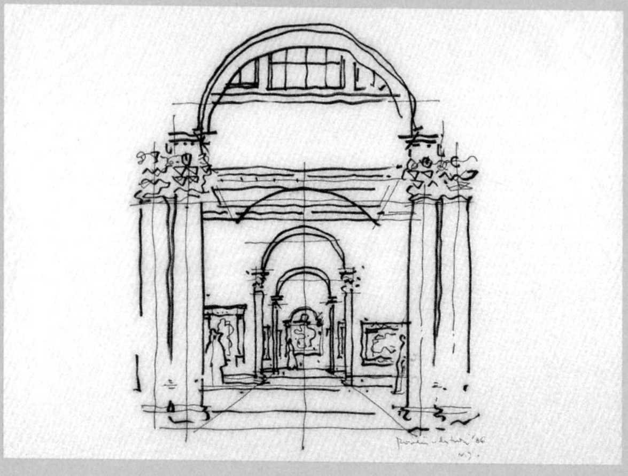

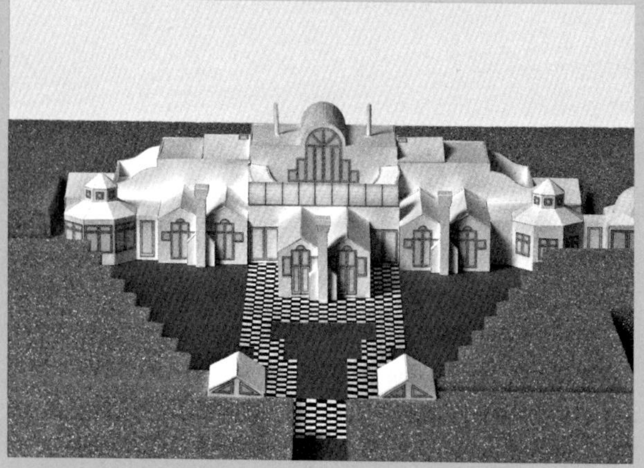

Fig. 1. Robert Venturi, National Gallery, London, Sainsbury Wing, sketch, 1986
Fig. 2. Stanley Tigerman, Bloch Residence, Highland Park, Illinois, site model, built 1982

1838 building. Tigerman's 7,000-square-foot Bloch Residence makes direct links to modernist architect Le Corbusier's concept of architecture as a machine in the garden.[8] The symmetrical facade breaks from the modernist idea that form follows function, while the use of the grid and references to classical architecture are apparent throughout the project.[9]

Architects in every era have attempted to capture and synthesize the rich lineage of styles and approaches that has been passed down. Fragments come together to create new movements, while looking to the past helps to illuminate dominant themes. This is expressed in

Bureau Spectacular

Drawings by Jimenez Lai, 2011–2014

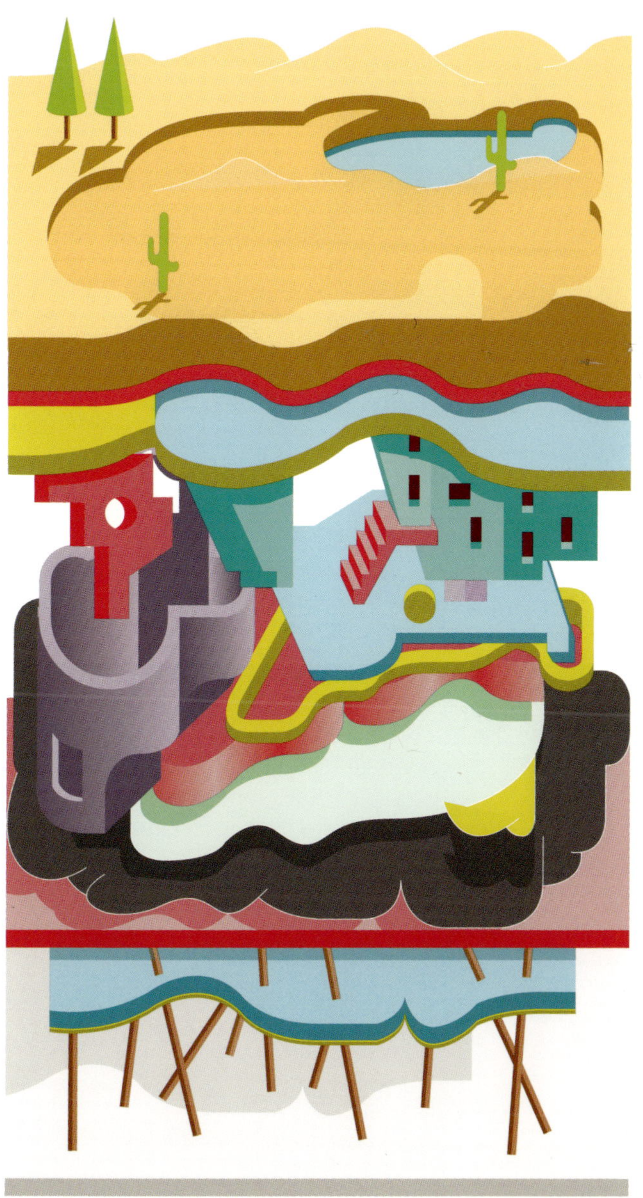

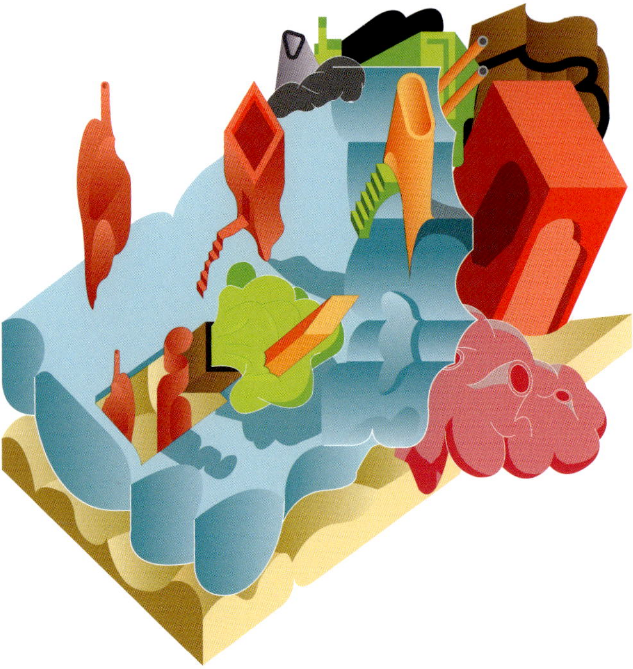

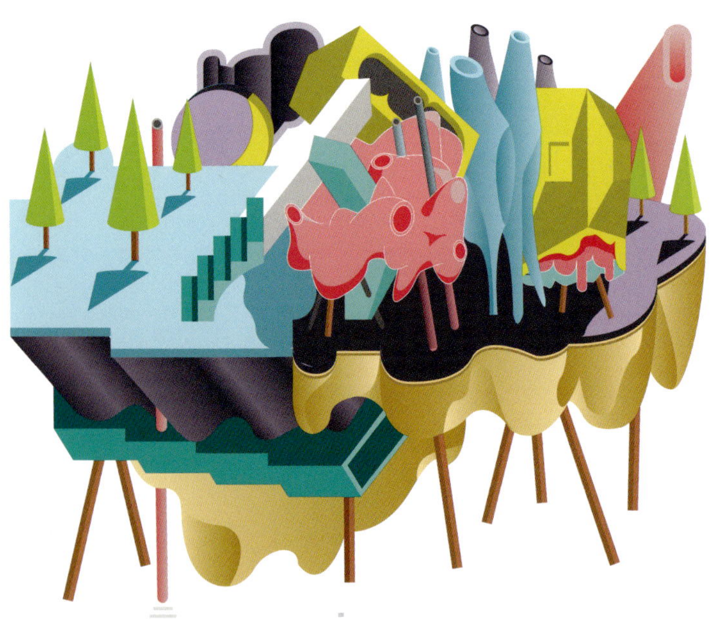

Bureau Spectacular / Jimenez Lai, assisted by Ed Crooks, *S'more with Sprinkles*, 2014

Bureau Spectacular / Jimenez Lai, assisted by Ed Crooks, *Villa dall'Ava and Parc de la Villette on a Roof*, 2014

Preceding page: Bureau Spectacular / Jimenez Lai, assisted by Ed Crooks, *Frankenstein Studies: Stacked Landscapes (MVRDV)*, 2014

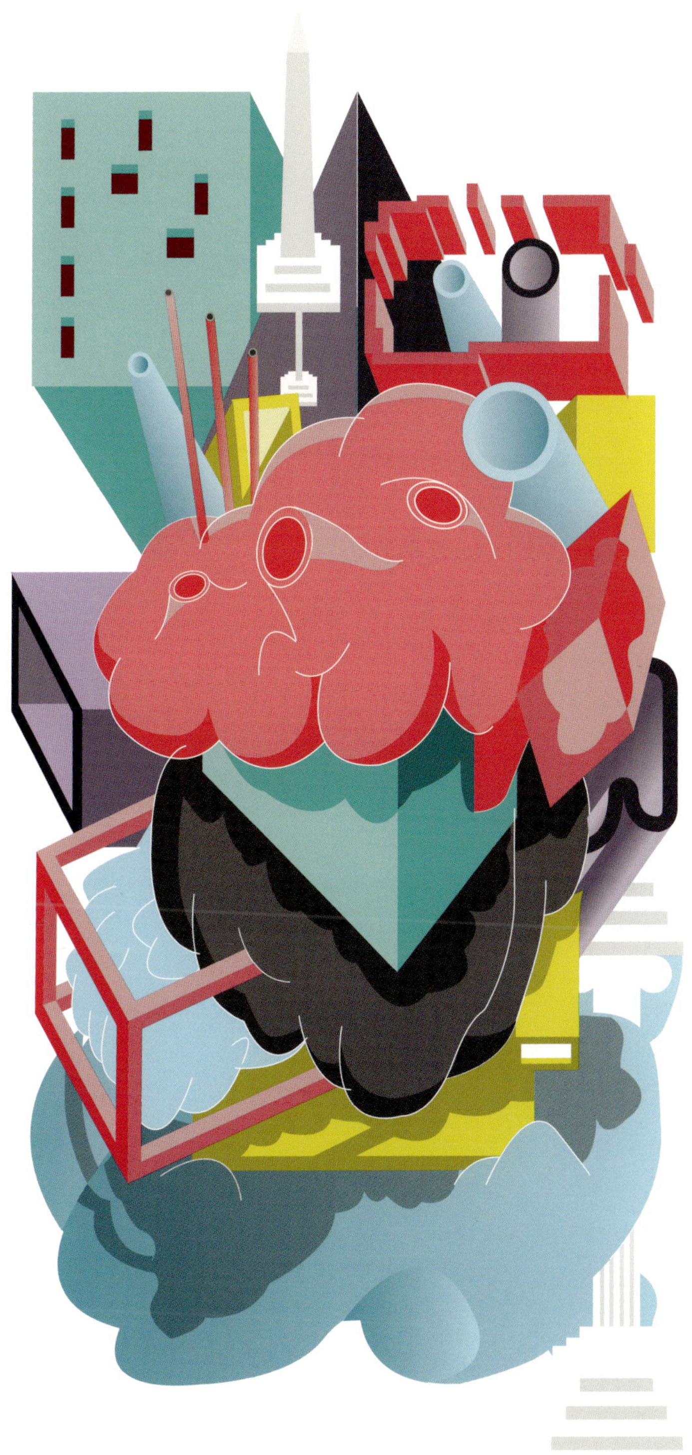

Bureau Spectacular / Jimenez Lai, assisted by Ed Crooks, *Mess Is More*, 2014

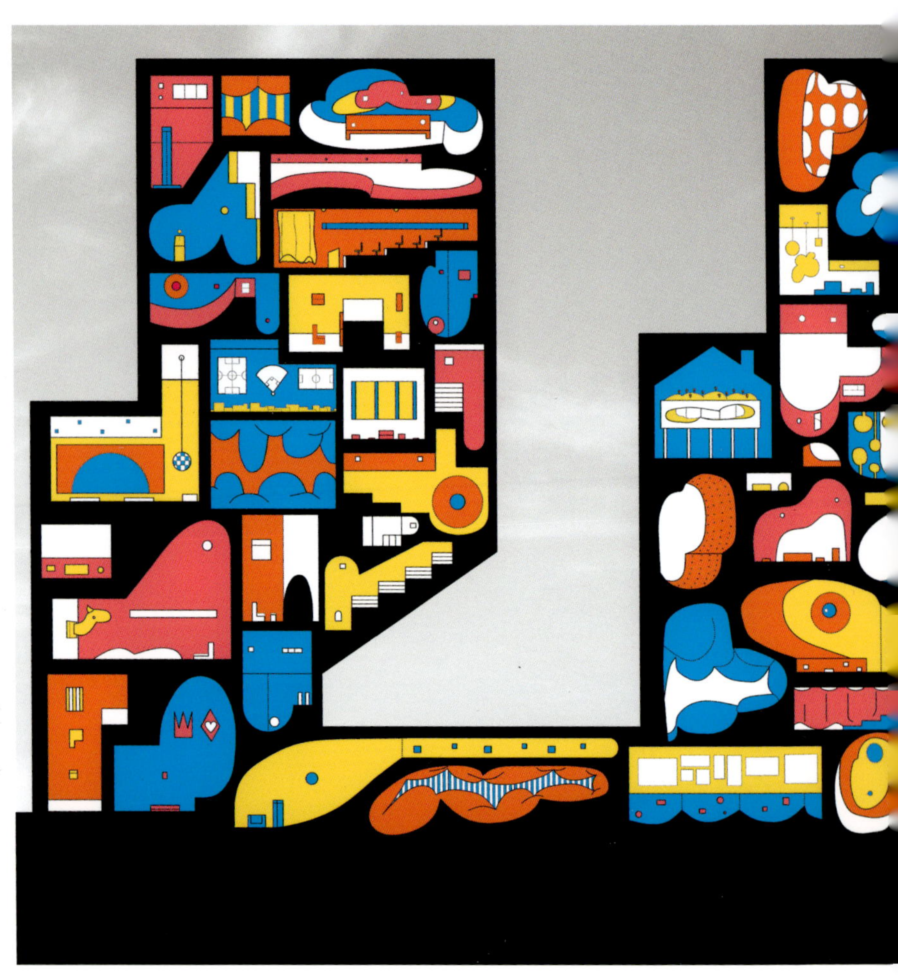

Bureau Spectacular / Jimenez Lai, assisted by Senaid Selcin and Frank Gossage, *Cartoonish Metropolis*, 2011

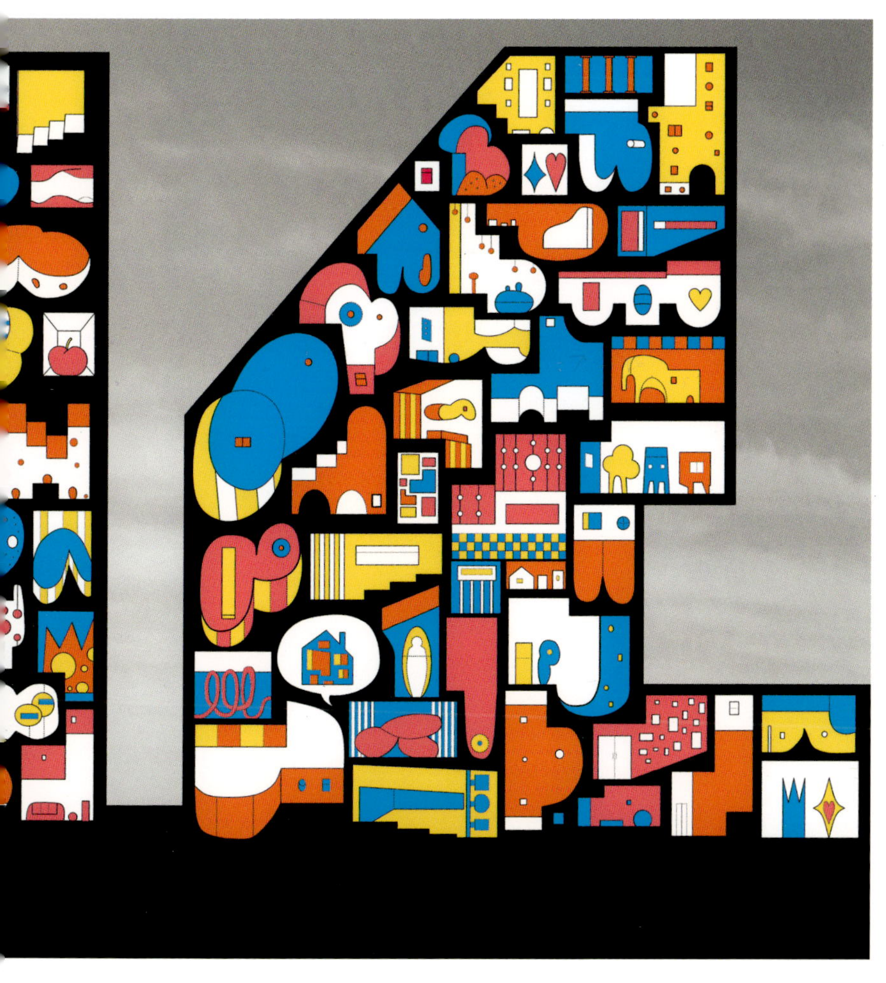

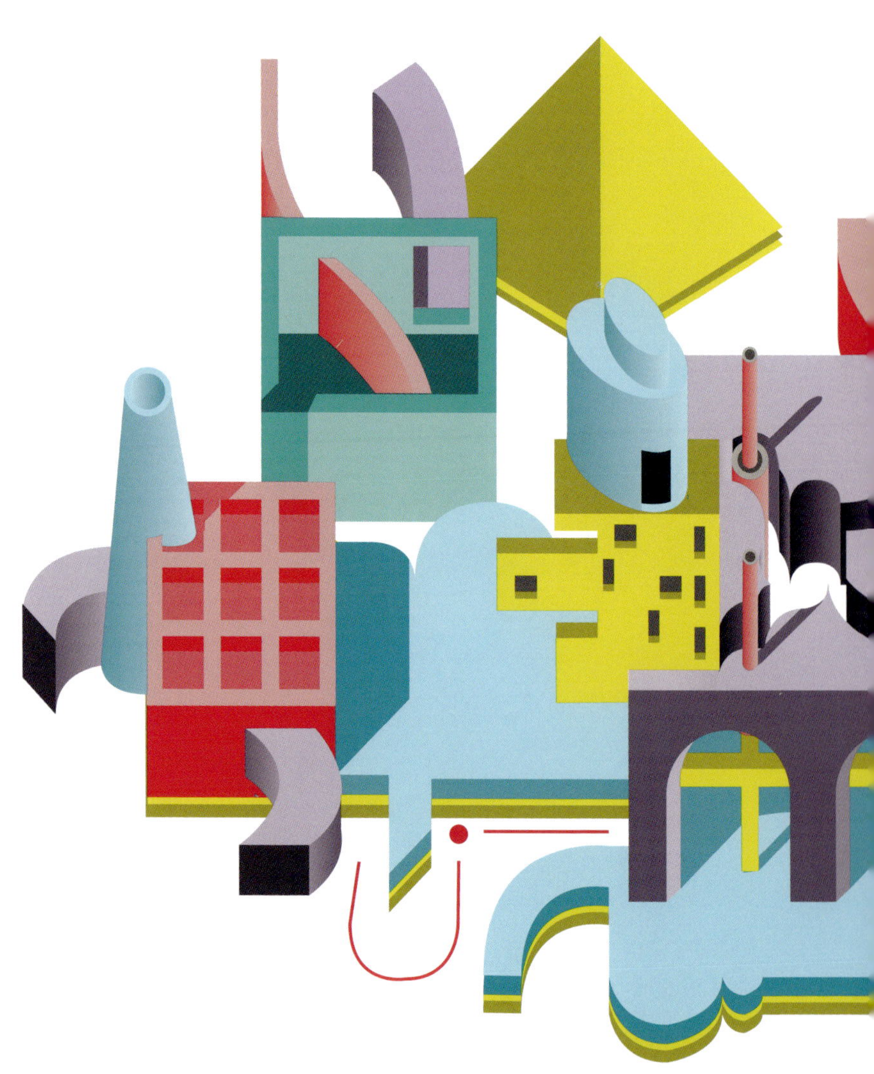

Bureau Spectacular / Jimenez Lai, assisted by Ed Crooks, *Tschumi Transcripts*, 2014

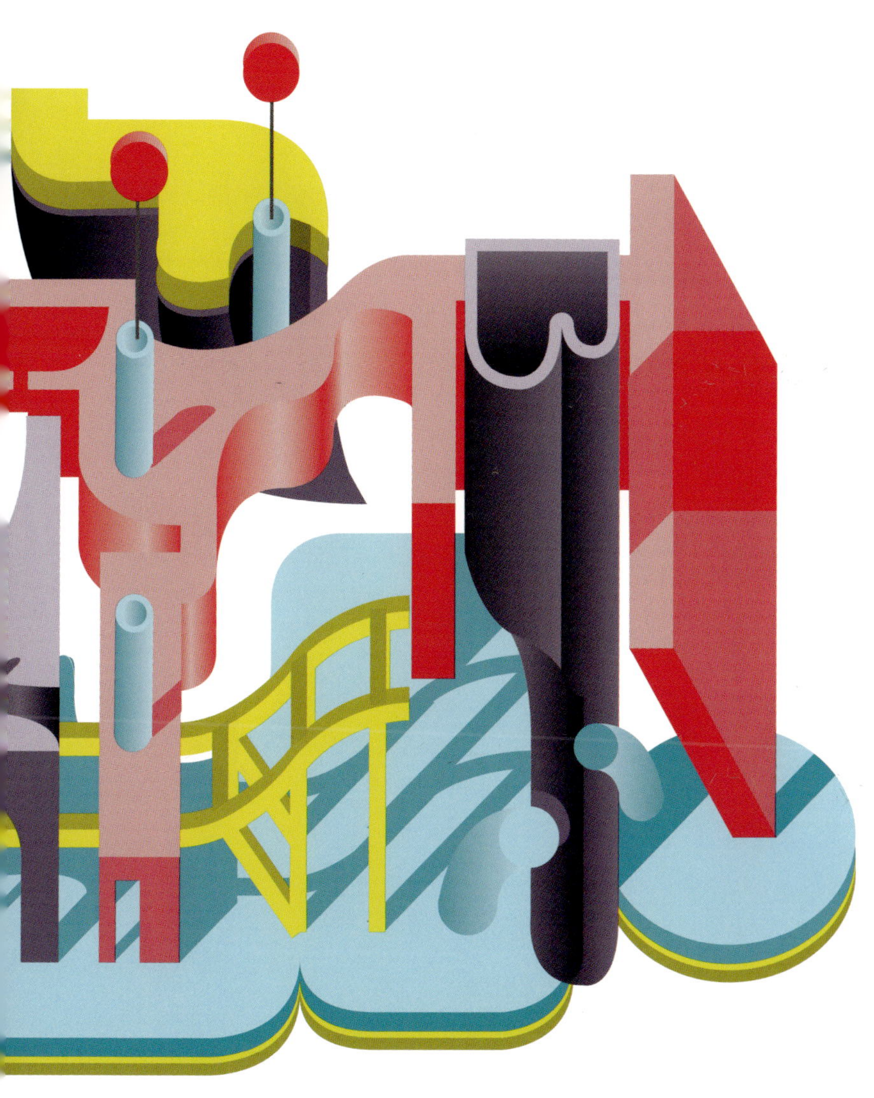

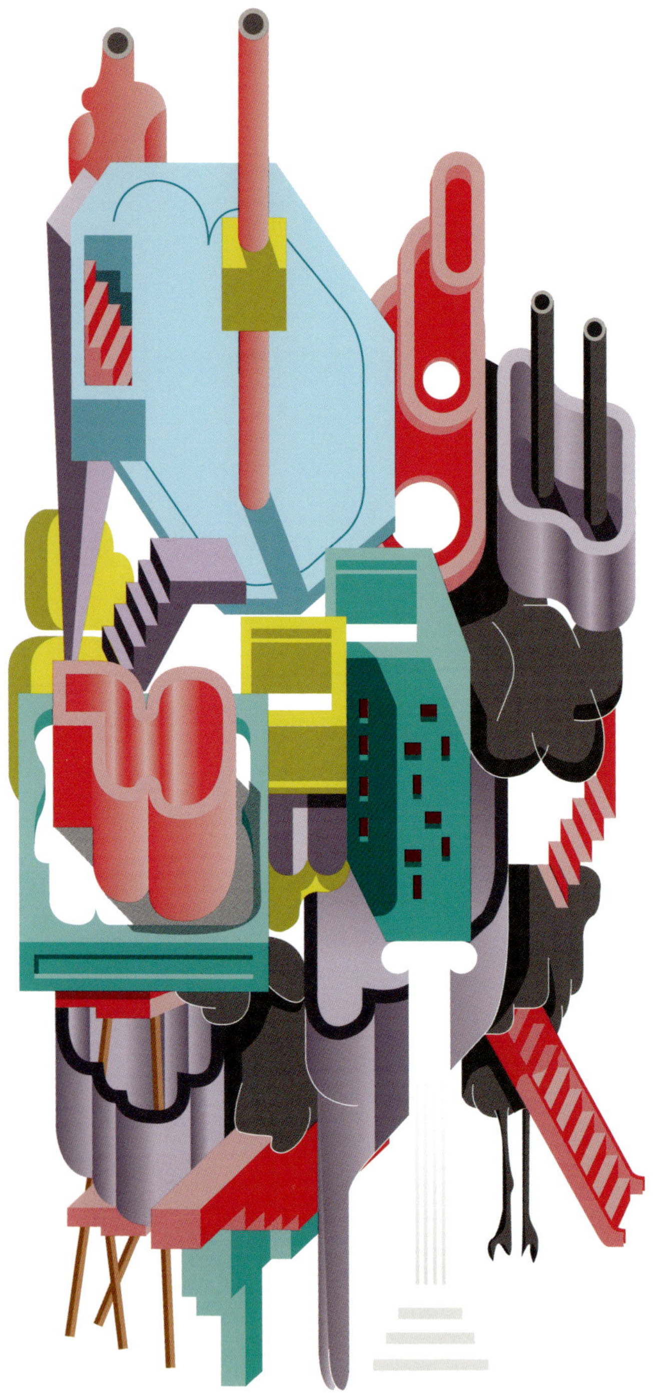

Bureau Spectacular / Jimenez Lai, assisted by Ed Crooks, *I Miss Chicago*, 2014

Charles Jencks's 1973 *Evolutionary Tree of Postmodern Architecture, 1920–1970* (fig. 3) and his updated version from 2000, *The Century Is Over, Evolutionary Tree of Twentieth-Century Architecture* (fig. 4), in which he not only attempted to identify and chart the various historical movements, but also revealed an intensified multiplicity and diversity of work at the turn of the twenty-first century. With each movement, there is a rethinking of the past—whether an overt reference is made or a precedent is used as a more nuanced point of departure. This ongoing process of looking back to the past in order to understand the pluralism that has evolved over time provides a context for developing work through a contemporary lens.

Recently, architects and theorists have noted a reemergence of this engagement with history, attributing it to a data-saturated culture paired with new ways to both disseminate and synthesize those data. Describing architects they defined as "New Ancients," theorist Dora Epstein Jones and architect Bryony Roberts identified this renewed interest in history as an "impudent stance," which is revealed in "a thousand tiny conscious ways of converting the terms of history into contemporary possibility. A 'new history' is nowhere near as reckless as imagining that architecture could exist without any precedents, nor does it fall into the traps of faithful reproduction or flippant sampling. Instead, we offer an alternate path to discovery through genealogical manipulation, one that has been latent in architecture all along."[10] This emergence of and reliance on history, however, is hardly novel, as critic Hal Foster noted: "My point is a basic one: dialectically—which is to say, necessarily and in spite of itself—neoconservative postmodernism is revealed by the very cultural moment it would otherwise flee. In turn, this moment is revealed to be marked not by a renascence of style, but by its implosion in pastiche; not by a return of a sense of history, but by its erosion; and not by a rebirth of the artist/architect as *auteur*, but by the death of the author as origin and center of meaning."[11] This superficial application, as pastiche or erosion of substance, that Foster cited positions history as destructive to the discipline. Yet the way the practitioners studied in this catalogue use history differs greatly: identifying its productive value as a substantive component of their thinking, and rooting a very contemporary approach—through both construction of ideas and communication—in the foundations of the field of architecture.

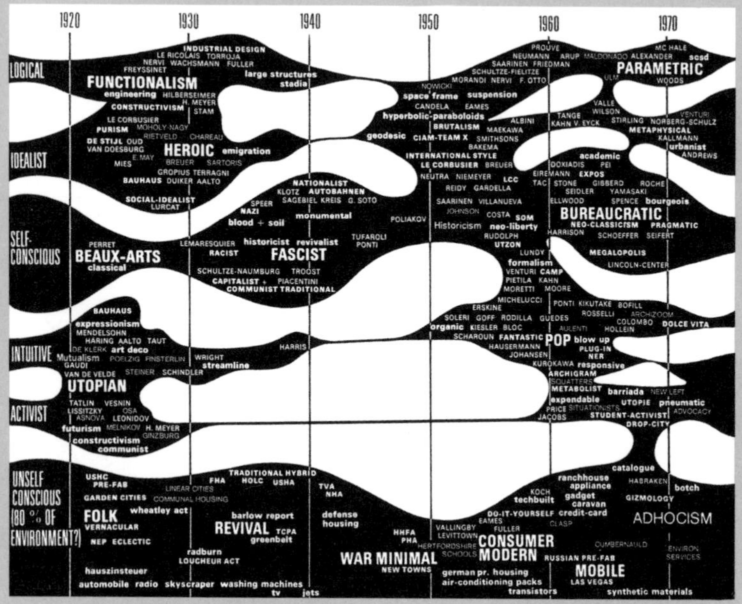

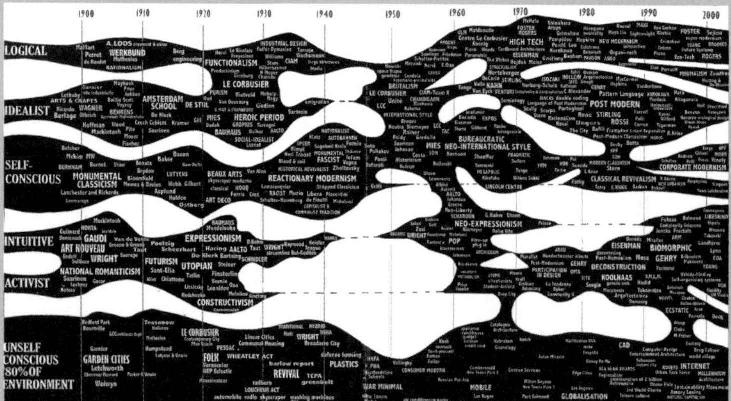

Fig. 3. Charles Jencks, *Evolutionary Tree of Postmodern Architecture, 1920–1970*, 1973

Fig. 4. Charles Jencks, *The Century Is Over, Evolutionary Tree of Twentieth-Century Architecture*, 2000

Conversations in Context

As a backdrop for the five case studies, *Chatter* includes a selection of work from the architecture and design collection at the Art Institute of Chicago. These examples help establish the context for conversations within the discipline that are embedded in and formulated through the work that architects produce, as they develop an approach to a project, contextualize their solutions, or expand on existing ideas. Stuart Cohen's architectural model Kindergarten Chats (1976; fig. 5), for example, was created in direct response to a 1918 text of the same title by Louis Sullivan.[12] Comprising fifty-two chapters structured around a hypothetical dialogue between a master and a student about an ideal architecture, Sullivan's book proposed that architecture should be an easily readable sign—that the building itself should indicate its use. Cohen articulated this with a simple house-like gesture in the postmodern front facade of his model. Though his piece relates to Sullivan's ideas as put forth in *Kindergarten Chats*, it emphasizes formal signs both as a reference to history and as a symbolic indicator of use, as seen in other postmodern projects such as Venturi and Scott Brown's Sainsbury Wing. In a similar vein, visionary architect Lauretta Vinciarelli's untitled drawings from 1981 (fig. 6) recombine and analyze the archetypal elements of the buildings in Marfa, Texas. These are part of a larger conceptual project Vinciarelli began in the late 1970s.[13] In this set of drawings, she abstracted and creatively reassembled basic architectural elements from the town's

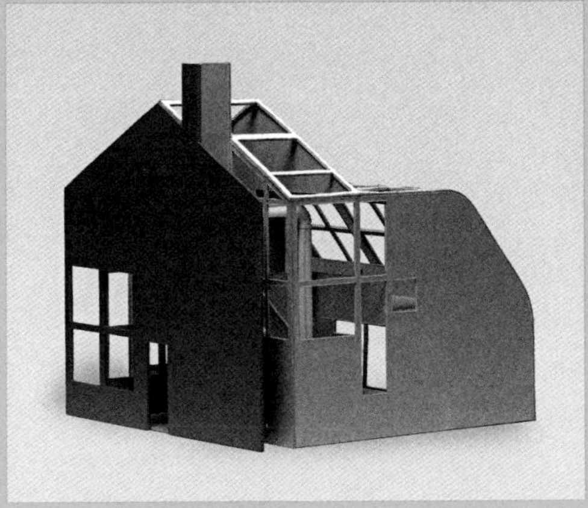

Fig. 5. Stuart Cohen, Kindergarten Chats, model, 1976

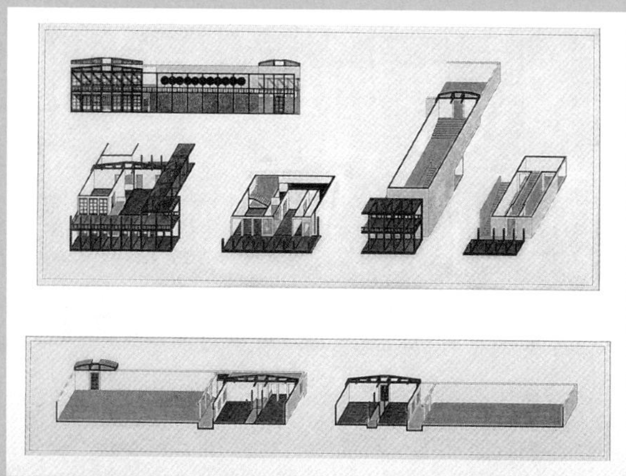

Fig. 6. Lauretta Vinciarelli, untitled drawings, 1981

distinct building style. The procession and space of an imagined building are depicted through axonometric projection, consistent scale, and parallelism. Completed at a moment when architectural discussions once again addressed issues of typology, Vinciarelli's work suggests and explores forms and ideas that propose an expanded language of architecture—one that breaks with and enlarges what many postmodern critics at the time claimed were the limited formal referents of modernism.

Architects have long used frameworks as conceptual guides for formal output. Walter Netsch, former principal at Skidmore, Owings & Merrill, is well known for field theory, an approach that is largely dependent on the use of geometry. By rotating square shapes, Netsch broke away from the modernist box to envision a complex field of grids as the basis for his designs. From this, shapes were built up to create distinct geometric forms. In the 1960s Netsch applied this technique to his designs for the Chicago campus of the University of Illinois, including the Behavioral Sciences Building, which he later expanded on in his late entry for the Chicago Tribune Tower competition (figs. 7, 8).[14] The notion of the field in architecture was later taken up by architect Stan Allen in his theory of field conditions, which accounts for the local context, rather than simply imposing a design on a site. With the aim of developing a cohesive relationship between the site and the architecture, Allen moved away from historical methods: "Field conditions oppose conventional Modernist modes of composition as much as [they oppose] classical rules of composition. The

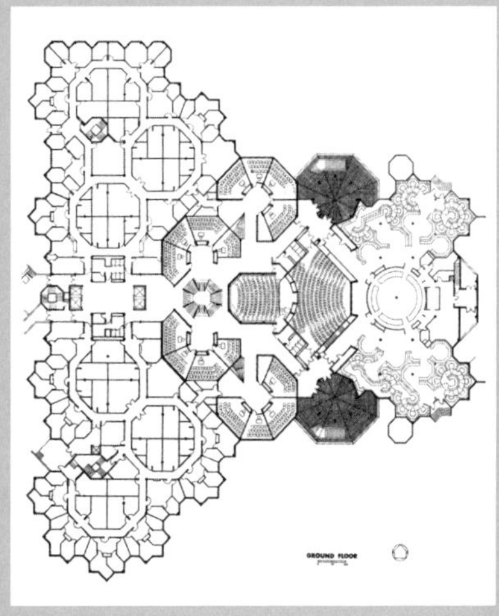

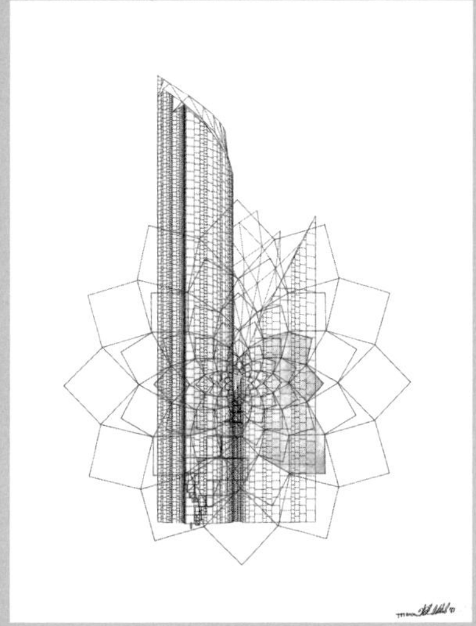

Fig. 7. Skidmore, Owings & Merrill / Walter Netsch, University of Illinois at Chicago, Behavioral Sciences Building, floor plan, 1968

Fig. 8. Skidmore, Owings & Merrill / Walter Netsch, Chicago Tribune Tower II, A Field Theory Butterfly Tower in the Chrysanthemum Field, 1981

provisionality of the whole undermines the classical aspiration to totality; the self-similarity of the parts and the intricacy of connection work against Modernist fragmentation. In the field condition, overall form emerges out of conditions established locally."[15] In Allen's 2010 competition entry for the New Maribor Art Gallery (figs. 9, 10), a cultural complex in Maribor, Slovenia, the form of the building is derived from an aggregation of pentagonal shapes supported by a single, treelike radiating column. What resulted from this approach is a continuous and flexible gallery space in the interior of the project, while

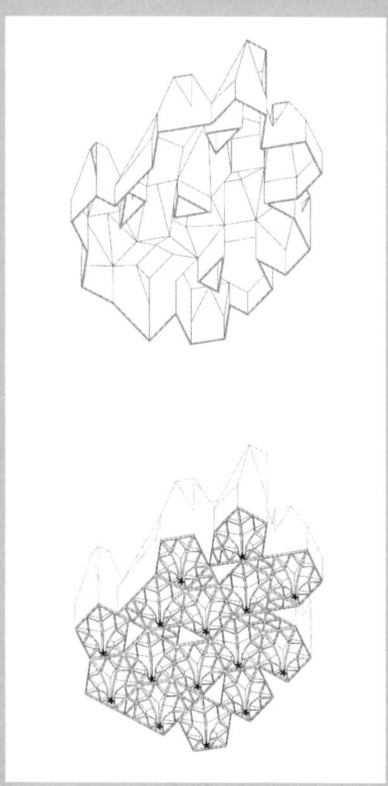

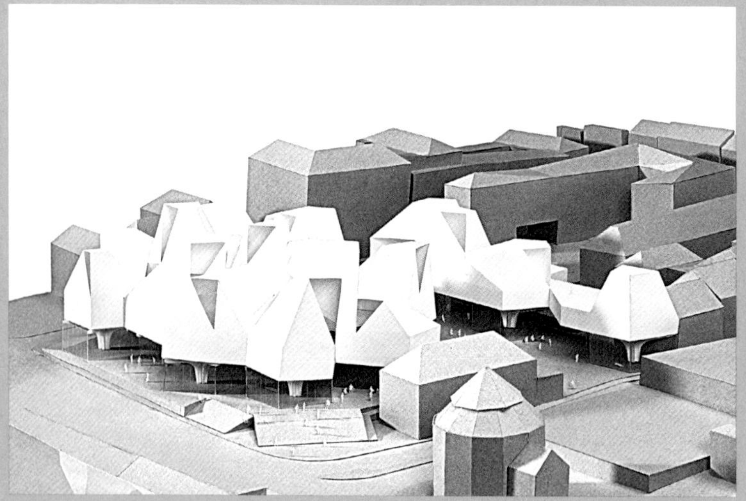

Fig. 9. Stan Allen Architect, New Maribor Art Gallery, structural assembly drawing, 2010

Fig. 10. Stan Allen Architect, New Maribor Art Gallery, site model, 2010

on the exterior, the articulated volume of the building relates to the scale and shapes of the nearby architecture, both announcing the museum's presence and linking it to the fabric of the city. Allen's antihierarchical design process—developed several decades after Netsch's field theory—reveals his relationship to the discipline of architecture as one that breaks away from previous movements, employing geometry to create a specific connection to the use, site, and local context of a project.

The passage of time provides the kind of perspective that allows these types of conversations to emerge, while also changing the way architects work and think and the tools that are available to them. Beyond the discipline of architecture itself, cultural, social, and technological advances equally incite these conversations. In the late 1980s and early 1990s, the Digital Revolution transformed the practice of architecture in multiple ways, including the emergence of the "paperless studio."[16] During this period, architects explored technology and digital tools intensively, not merely as an aid to production but also as conceptual devices that stimulated a new formal direction in the profession. A handful of pioneers, including Frank Gehry, Peter Eisenman, and Greg Lynn, embraced new computer programs as generative tools that revolutionized the discipline by giving architects new ways to manipulate data, generate form, and test multiple iterations of a design.

Although technology was an impetus for much of the work of this period and allowed new formal possibilities, it can be argued that architects such as Eisenman and Lynn were "digital" before the Digital Revolution took hold in the field. As underlined by architectural historian Mario Carpo, "computers *per se* do not impose shapes, nor do they articulate aesthetic preferences. One can use computers to design boxes or folds, indifferently."[17] In the early years of digital technology, many architects were working alongside, and often faster than, computers. It was the mind of the architect that maneuvered the computer and the corresponding output. In 1992 Lynn developed a conceptual project, Stranded Sears Tower (figs. 11, 12), as his last fully handmade design; in it he separated and dissected the nine vertical structural tubes of Chicago's Sears Tower (now Willis Tower) into individual strands and then reoriented them horizontally. Lynn's project reinvented the form of Skidmore, Owings & Merrill's 1973 skyscraper (until 1998 the tallest building in the world) from a rigid,

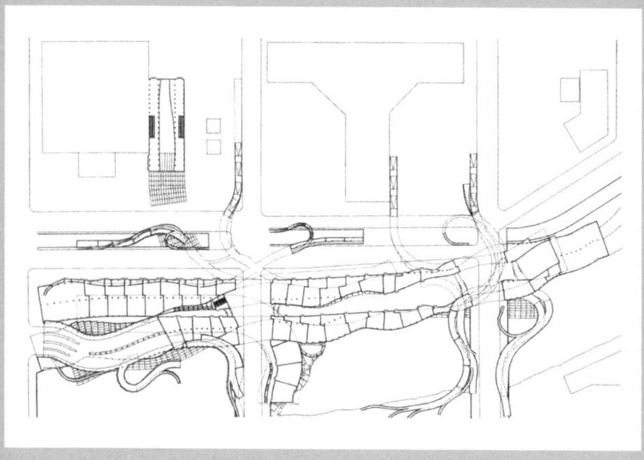

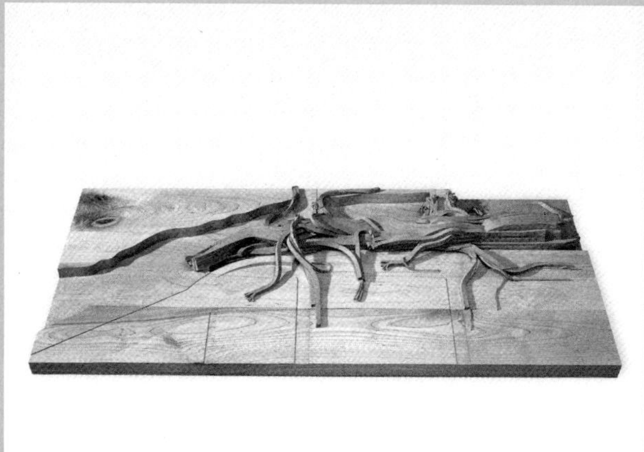

Fig. 11. Greg Lynn, Stranded Sears Tower, plan drawing, 1992

Fig. 12. Greg Lynn, Stranded Sears Tower, model, 1992

vertical tower to a horizontal, supple, fluid architecture, proposing an alternative way the building could engage with the city. Not only conversing with the iconic skyscraper, Lynn spoke also to new possibilities for form and ways of working in the discipline that would soon be guided by emerging digital technologies. Digital architecture would come to be characterized by projects such as Xefirotarch's Sur, Long Island City, New York (2005; fig. 13), in which Hernán Díaz Alonso demonstrated the generative capabilities of digital tools through the use of parametric design in his winning proposal for the sixth annual MoMA PS1 Young Architects Program, a competition that selects emerging architects to design and build a temporary outdoor pavilion at MoMA PS1. The glossy, skeletal form of the physical model for

Formlessfinder

Tent Pile Pavilion, 2013

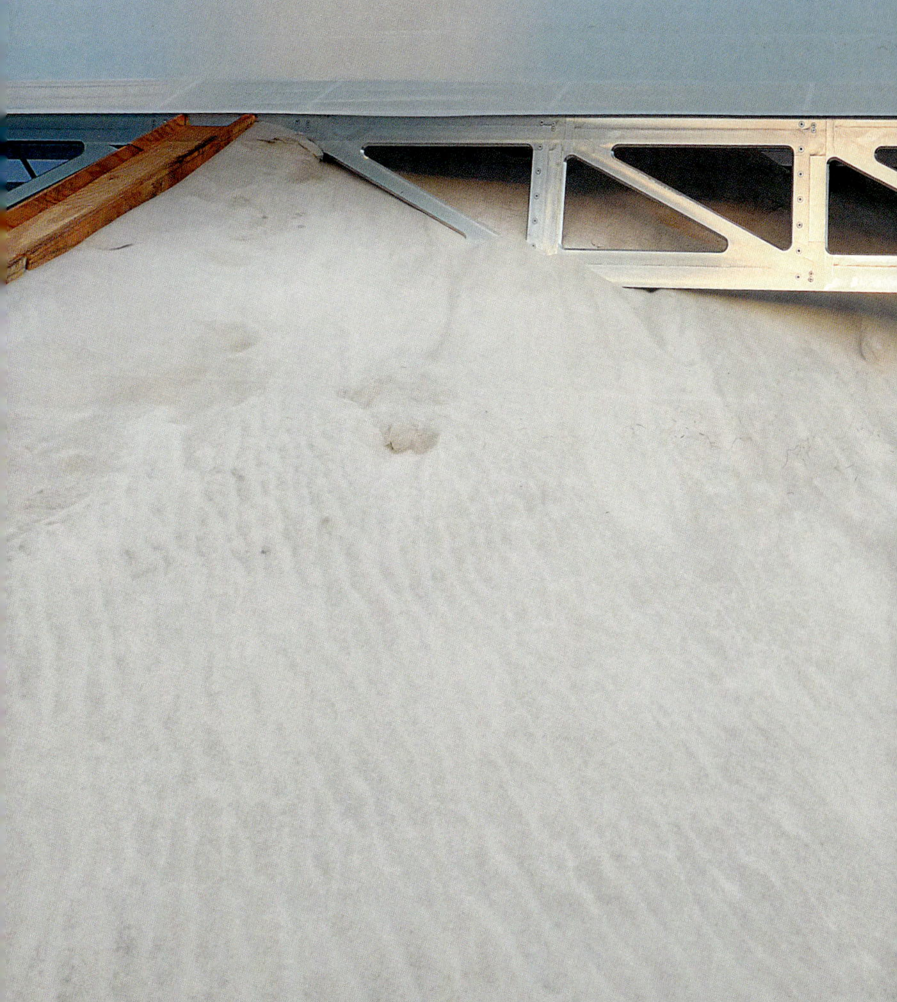

formlessfinder

FIND

over 480 210 operations

Choose a Definition

Name

- AS FOUND
- STRUCTURE
- MAPS
- PURCHASE ORDERS
- LOGISTICS
- TEXTS
- HISTORY
  - HIST OF FORMLESS
  - NEAR MISS
    - ANCIENT ✓
    - CLASSICAL
    - BAROQUE
    - MANNERISM
    - EXPRESSIONISM
    - MODERN
    - POSTMODERN
    - COTEMPORARY
- THEORY
  - TEXT
  - DIAGRAMS
  - REVISED 01
  - REVISED 02
  - REVISED 03
  - REVISED 04
  - REVISED 05
- AS BUILT

FIND | EXPERIMENTS | PROJECTS | INTERVIEWS | ABOUT

Near Misses_Platonic_Aristotelian_Form

340 BC -

Near Misses

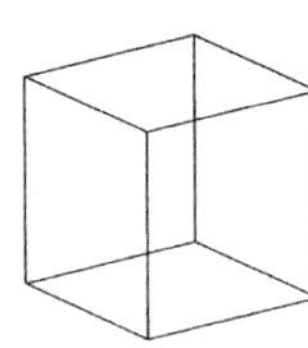

Platonic vs. Aristotelian Form

Near Misses

Form not only as old as architecture, but as old as Western thought. Since the beginning of philosophy, there are certain classes of matter that people haven't been able to conceptualize: these are formless things. Recall, for example, a suggestive quote from the Platonic dialogue Parmenides: A pupil asked: "Socrates..., such things as hair, mud, dirt, or anything else which is vile and paltry; would you suppose that each of these has an idea distinct from the actual objects with which we come into contact, or not?" And Socrates replied: "Certainly not... I am afraid that there would be an absurdity in assuming any idea of them."

As is well known, then, without an idea, you can't have a form. In other words, one of the most influential understandings of form we inherited from antiquity excluded raw matter. Formless matter is something that we have always had trouble thinking about, that has always been outside of philosophy. But our goal is not simply to escape into the formless. Or force architecture to abandon form altogether. Instead, we're looking for a formless sweet spot. There are a range of options between the abstract rigidity of form (the Platonic cube, say) and the utter abjection of raw material (the mud puddle). That's why this sculpture by the artist Lucio Fontana is one of our favorite artworks. It's a simultaneity, a both/and: a cube and a pile of shit. This sense of simultaneity is crucial to the formless, which isn't about a dialectic or an absence, but rather always about an interaction.

Of course, a more material understanding of form was provided by Plato's pupil, Aristotle. But his teleological theory, where form grows from material, and material is animated by a will to form, form is equally problematic. Yet it was incredibly influential, influencing centuries of art history, early theories of evolutionary biology, and even contemporary computational design, where proponents of scripting and parametric like to talk about "smart materials" or "smart particles"—the fantasy that form grows and self-assembles, or that "form is in the algorithm."

In the end, there have historically been two ways of linking form and material—you either place form totally outside of the material world, or you claim that material always has the seeds of formal order within it. Either way, you suppress raw matter. The formless, as an approach, is about enabling a more direct engagement with materiality.

Formlessfinder: Catalog of Near Misses

Formlessfinder: Catalog of Near Misses

formlessfinder

FIND

over 480 210 operations

Choose a Definition

Name

- AS FOUND
  - PRE-EXISTING COND.
  - IMAGES
  - TYPOLOGIES
  - EVENTS
  - STRUCTURES
    - AGGREGATE
      - SAND 01
      - SAND 02
      - SAND 03 ✓
    - COMPOSITE
    - INFORMAL
  - SCALE
- STRUCTURE
  - PILES
  - JOINED
  - UNJOINED
  - COMPRESSION
  - UNCLASSIFIED
  - BUNDLED
- MAPS
- PURCHASE ORDERS
- LOGISTICS
- TEXTS
- HISTORY
  - HIST OF FORMLESS
  - NEAR MISS
    - ANCIENT
    - CLASSICAL
    - BAROQUE
    - MANNERISM
    - EXPRESSIONISM
    - MODERN
    - POSTMODERN
    - COTEMPORARY
- THEORY
- AS BUILT

FIND | EXPERIMENTS | PROJECTS | INTERVIEWS | ABOUT

Found Condition

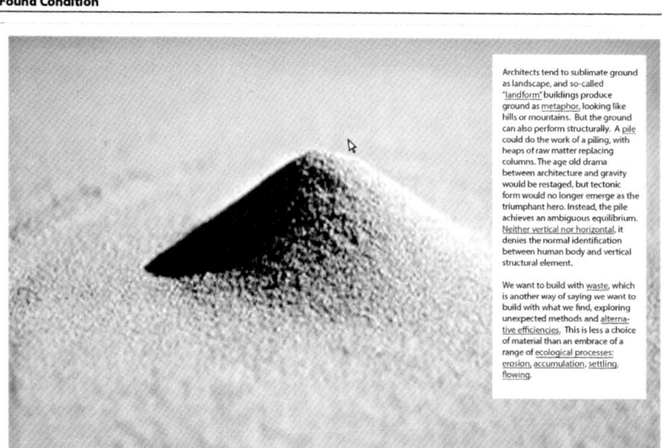

Architects tend to sublimate ground as landscape, and so-called "landform" buildings produce ground as metaphor, looking like hills or mountains. But the ground can also perform structurally. A pile could do the work of a piling, with heaps of raw matter replacing columns. The age old drama between architecture and gravity would be restaged, but tectonic form would no longer emerge as the triumphant hero. Instead, the pile achieves an ambiguous equilibrium. Neither vertical nor horizontal, it denies the normal identification between human body and vertical structural element.

We want to build with waste, which is another way of saying we want to build with what we find, exploring unexpected methods and alternative efficiencies. This is less a choice of material than an embrace of a range of ecological processes: erosion, accumulation, settling, flowing.

formlessfinder

FIND

over 480 210 operations

Choose a Definition

Name

- ⊞ AS FOUND
- ⊟ STRUCTURE
  - ⊟ PILES
    - ⊟ LOADING
      - POINT LOAD
      - UNIFORM DIST ...
    - ⊟ EXT LOADING ✓
      - WIND
      - RAIN
  - JOINED
  - UNJOINED
  - COMPRESSION
  - UNCLASSIFIED
  - BUNDLED
- MAPS
- PURCHASE ORDERS
- ⊞ LOGISTICS
- TEXTS
- ⊟ HISTORY
  - HIST OF FORMLESS
  - ⊟ NEAR MISS
    - ANCIENT
    - CLASSICAL
    - BAROQUE
    - MANNERISM
    - EXPRESSIONISM
    - MODERN
    - POSTMODERN
    - COTEMPORARY
- ⊞ THEORY
- ⊞ AS BUILT

FIND | EXPERIMENTS | PROJECTS | INTERVIEWS | ABOUT

Wind Driven Profiles of Loose Agregate Sand

Profile 1

Profile 2

Profile 3

Profile 4

Profile 5

Profile 6

Legend:
Dune
Interdune
Crest-line
GPR profile
Superimposed dune

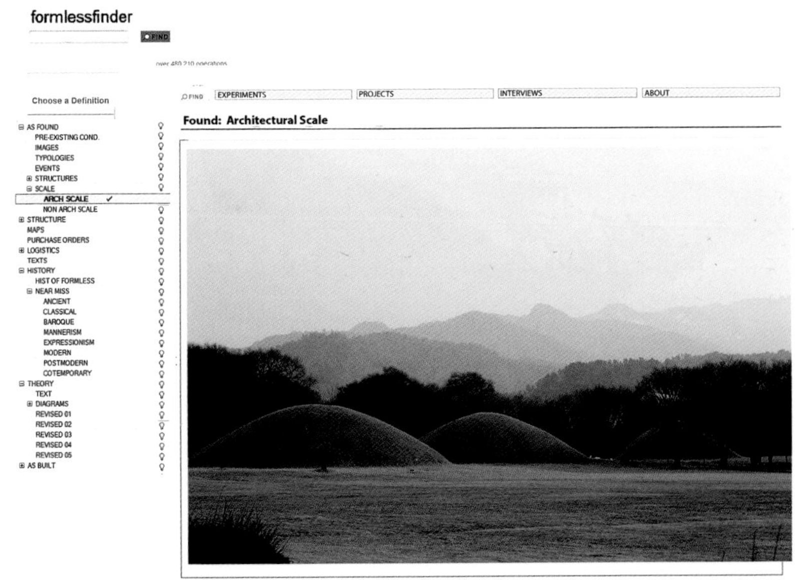

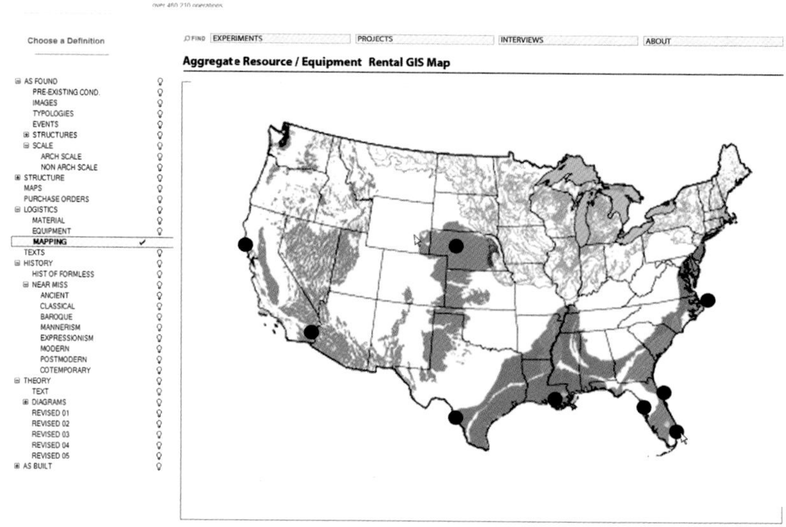
formlessfinder
FIND
Choose a Definition
FIND
EXPERIMENTS
PROJECTS
INTERVIEWS
ABOUT
Aggregate Resource / Equipment Rental GIS Map
AS FOUND
PRE-EXISTING COND.
IMAGES
TYPOLOGIES
EVENTS
STRUCTURES
SCALE
ARCH SCALE
NON ARCH SCALE
STRUCTURE
MAPS
PURCHASE ORDERS
LOGISTICS
MATERIAL
EQUIPMENT
MAPPING
TEXTS
HISTORY
HIST OF FORMLESS
NEAR MISS
ANCIENT
CLASSICAL
BAROQUE
MANNERISM
EXPRESSIONISM
MODERN
POSTMODERN
COTEMPORARY
THEORY
TEXT
DIAGRAMS
REVISED 01
REVISED 02
REVISED 03
REVISED 04
REVISED 05
AS BUILT

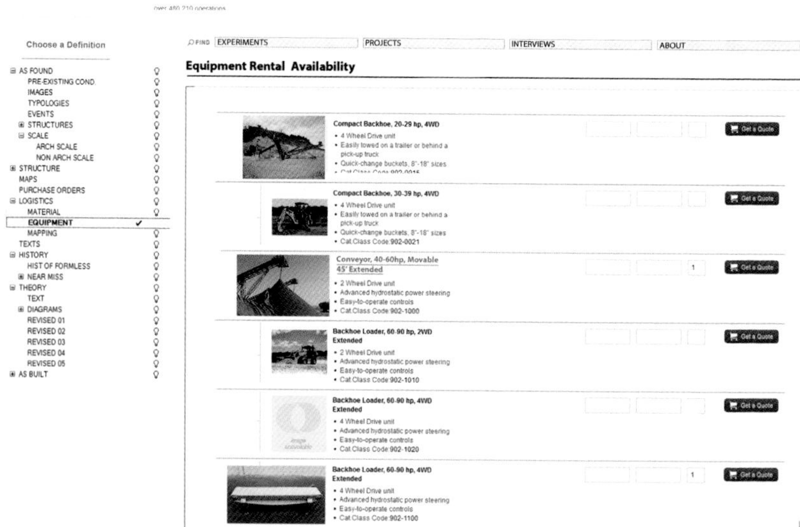
formlessfinder
FIND
Choose a Definition
FIND
EXPERIMENTS
PROJECTS
INTERVIEWS
ABOUT
Equipment Rental Availability
AS FOUND
PRE-EXISTING COND.
IMAGES
TYPOLOGIES
EVENTS
STRUCTURES
SCALE
ARCH SCALE
NON ARCH SCALE
STRUCTURE
MAPS
PURCHASE ORDERS
LOGISTICS
MATERIAL
EQUIPMENT
MAPPING
TEXTS
HISTORY
HIST OF FORMLESS
NEAR MISS
THEORY
TEXT
DIAGRAMS
REVISED 01
REVISED 02
REVISED 03
REVISED 04
REVISED 05
AS BUILT
Compact Backhoe, 20-29 hp, 4WD
• 4 Wheel Drive unit
• Easily towed on a trailer or behind a pick-up truck
• Quick-change buckets, 8"-18" sizes
Get a Quote
Compact Backhoe, 30-39 hp, 4WD
• 4 Wheel Drive unit
• Easily towed on a trailer or behind a pick-up truck
• Quick-change buckets, 8"-18" sizes
• Cat.Class Code:902-0021
Get a Quote
Conveyor, 40-60hp, Movable 45' Extended
• 2 Wheel Drive unit
• Advanced hydrostatic power steering
• Easy-to-operate controls
• Cat.Class Code:902-1000
1
Get a Quote
Backhoe Loader, 60-90 hp, 2WD Extended
• 2 Wheel Drive unit
• Advanced hydrostatic power steering
• Easy-to-operate controls
• Cat.Class Code:902-1010
Get a Quote
Backhoe Loader, 60-90 hp, 4WD Extended
• 4 Wheel Drive unit
• Advanced hydrostatic power steering
• Easy-to-operate controls
• Cat.Class Code:902-1020
Get a Quote
Backhoe Loader, 60-90 hp, 4WD Extended
• 4 Wheel Drive unit
• Advanced hydrostatic power steering
• Easy-to-operate controls
• Cat.Class Code:902-1100
1
Get a Quote

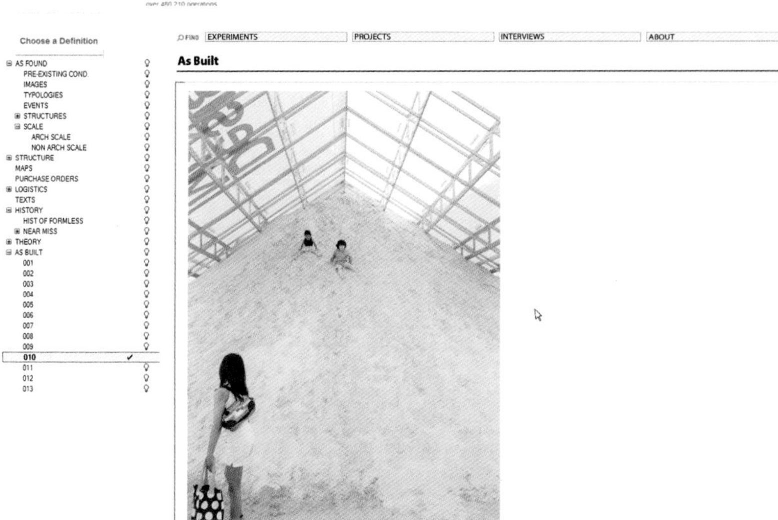

formlessfinder

FIND

Choose a Definition

FIND EXPERIMENTS | PROJECTS | INTERVIEWS | ABOUT

Revised Historical Diagram

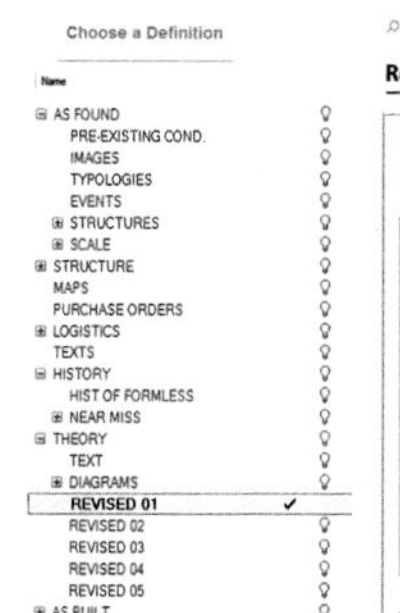

LoadTest_FoundCondition

Early in the development of modernism, nineteenth century theories of tectonics promoted the idea that making form was in itself the constitutive act of architecture. One of the founders of modern art and architectural history, Aloïs Riegl, characterized works of art and architecture as defined most fundamentally by a "will to form" (his notion of kunstwollen). Heinrich Wölfflin, another seminal figure in early art and architectural history, went so far as to claim that "the principle theme of architecture" is "a will that struggles to become form and has to overcome the resistance of a formless matter."

Raw matter has always been the basic building block of architecture, though it is always transformed through construction and fabrication. But perhaps it could finally be made into something besides form? After all, anything can perform structurally. Even crushed spiders, stacked high enough, could hold up a building.

"Will to form" was the first, and most common, English translation of Riegl's term, which is notoriously difficult to translate directly, and has been rendered more literally as a "will to art." For a full discussion of the difficulty in translating Riegl's terminology, see: Jacqueline E Jung, "Translator's Preface," in Aloïs Reigl, Historical Grammar of the Visual Arts (New York, NY: Zone Books, 2004), 37-50.

[2]Wölfflin first theorized architecture as an opposition between form and matter, and more specifically as the process of shaping matter into form, in his dissertation, first published in 1886. See: Heinrich Wölfflin, "Prolegomena to a Psychology of Architecture," in Empathy, Form, and Space: Problems in German Aesthetics, 1873-1893, ed. Harry Francis Mallgrave and Eleftherios Ikonomou (Santa Monica, CA: Getty Center for the History of Art, 1994), 159.

Formlessfinder: Projects

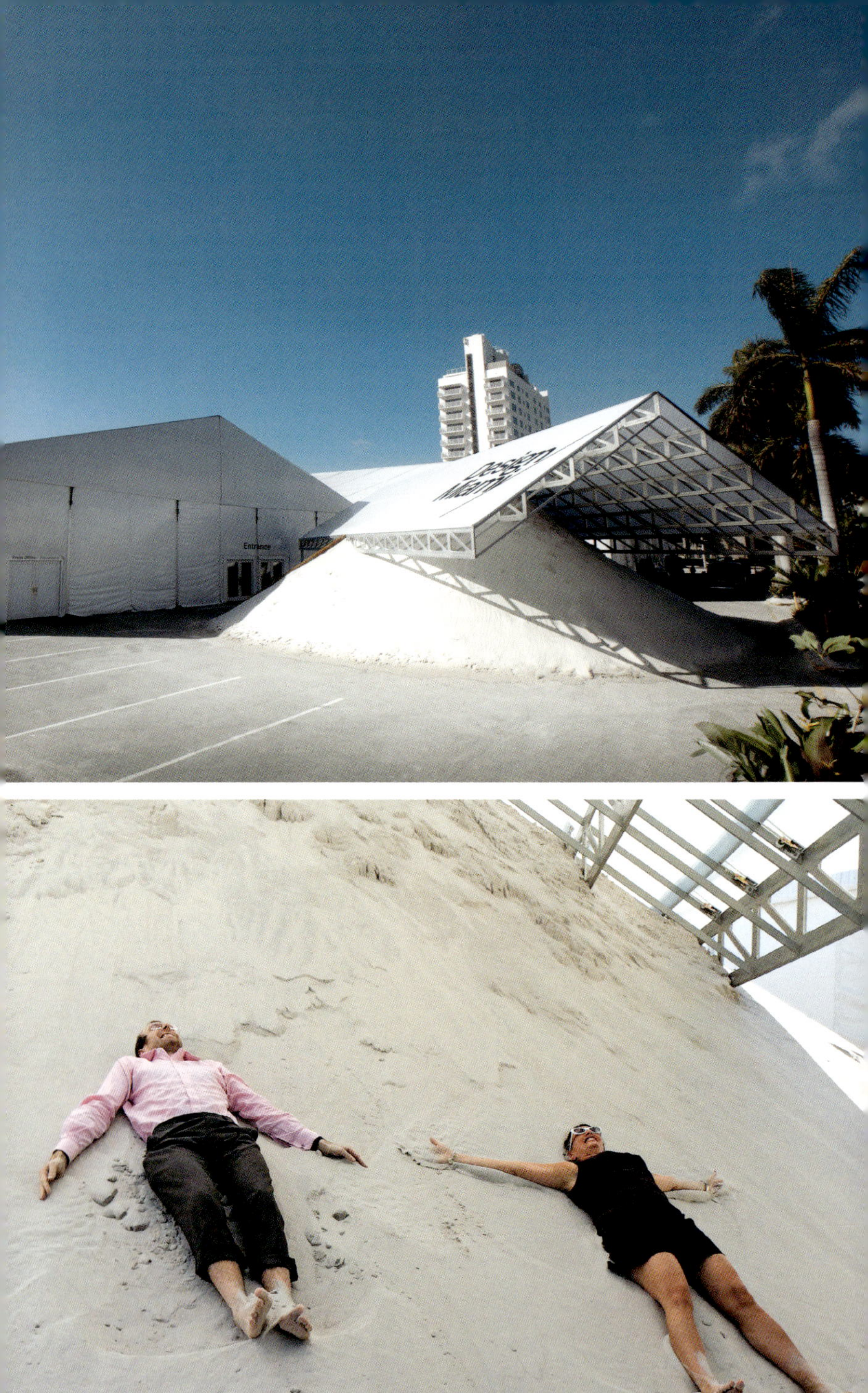
Entrance

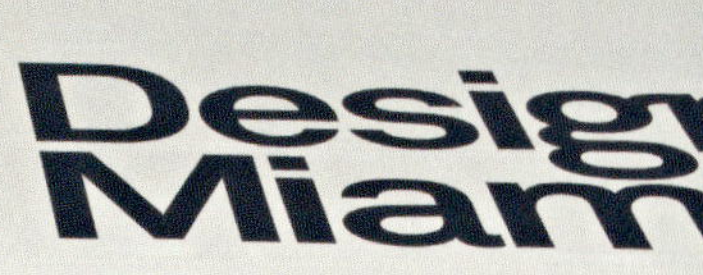

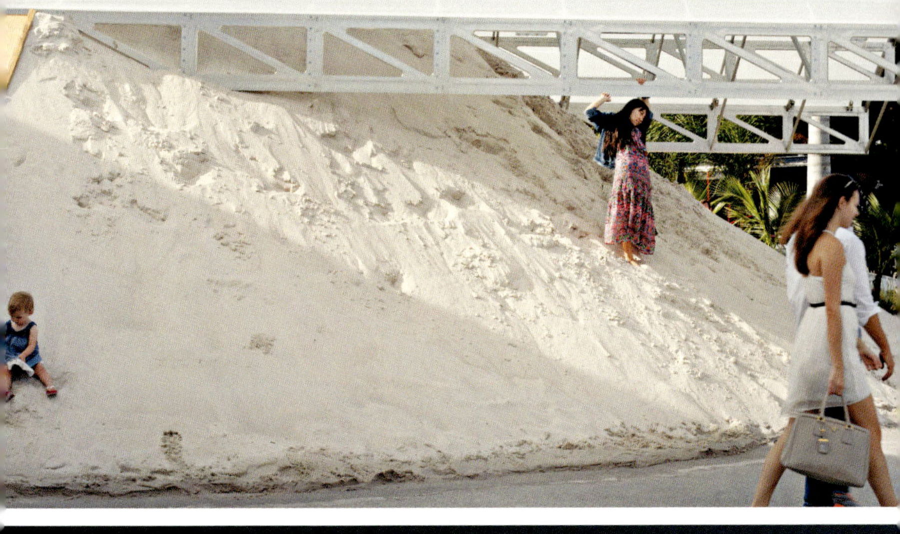

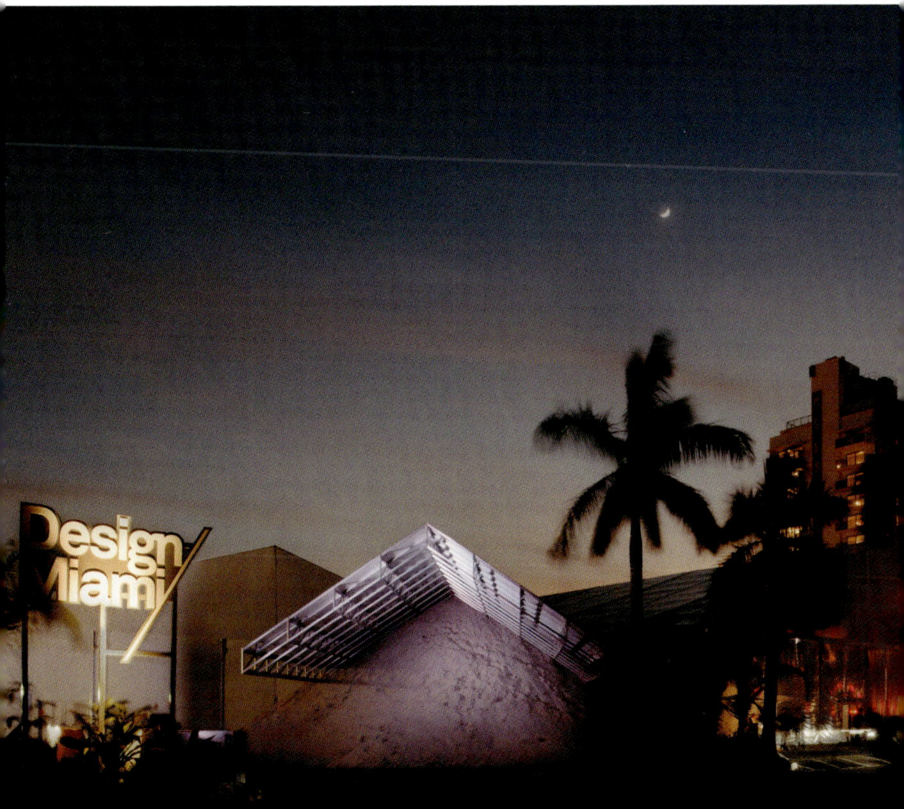

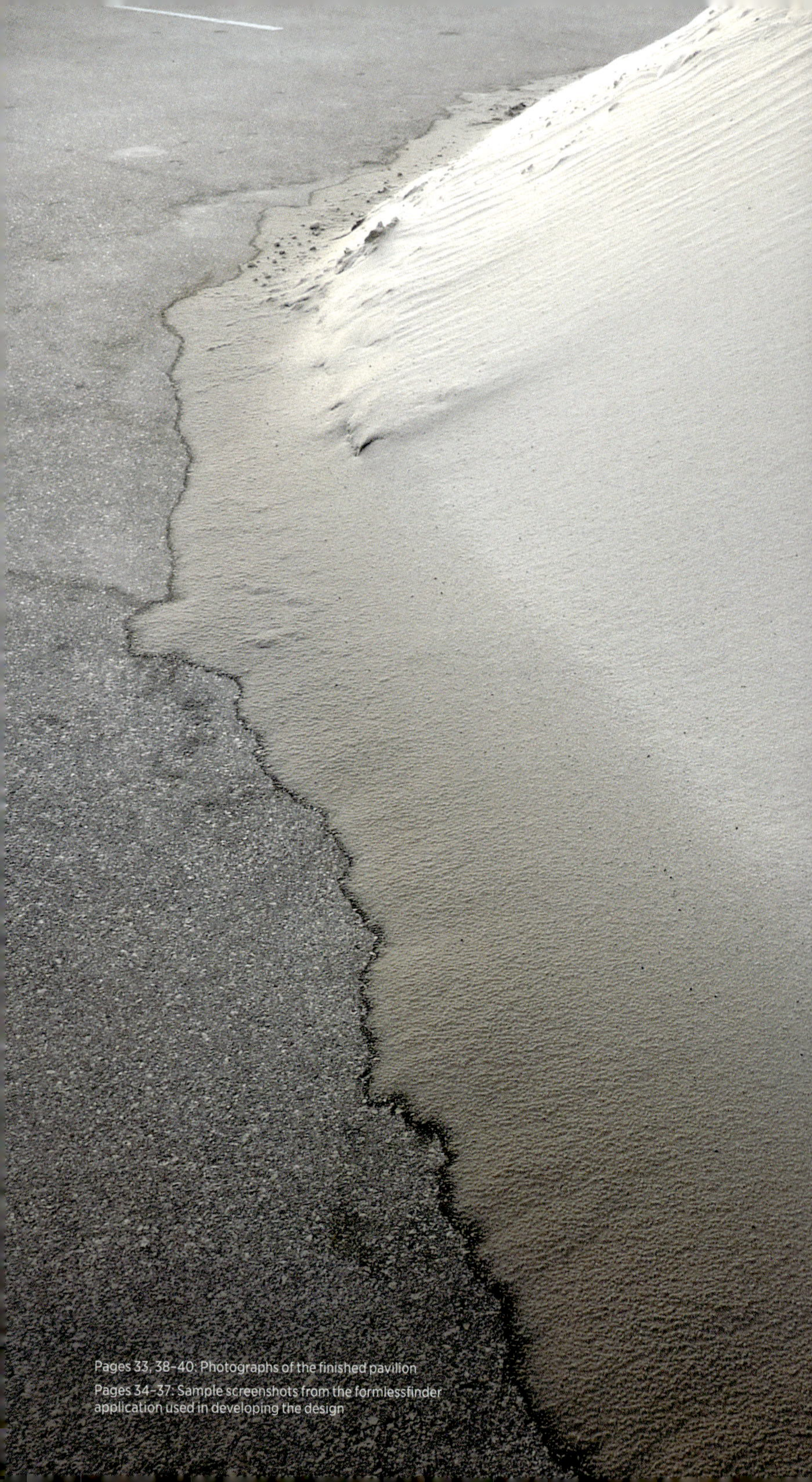

Pages 33, 38–40: Photographs of the finished pavilion

Pages 34–37: Sample screenshots from the formlessfinder application used in developing the design

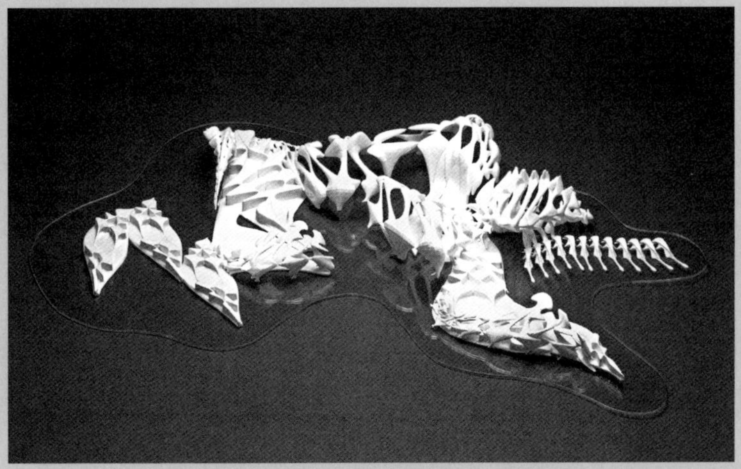

Fig. 13. Xefirotarch / Hernán Díaz Alonso, Sur, Long Island City, New York, model, 2005

Sur was a direct translation from a digital rendering to an object using 3-D printing. Owing to these technologies, Díaz Alonso's theories on architecture were able to take on physical form for the first time.

This seminal moment sparked optimistic conversations in architecture around the promises of "the digital," a term that originally carried futuristic overtones but has since been repositioned as belonging to the recent past.[18] The Digital Revolution may be over, but this recent history has had a huge impact on the professional and pedagogical landscape, producing a new paradigm and a generation of architects accustomed to a continuous flow of information and reliance on technology. Art critic Jonathan Crary has characterized the moment this way: "One of the most numbingly familiar assumptions in discussions of contemporary technological culture is that there has been an epochal shift in a relatively short period of time, in which new information and communication technologies have supplanted a broad set of older cultural forms. This historical break is described and theorized in various ways," one of which is a change "from a print-based culture to a global society unified by the instantaneous circulation of data and information."[19] This flood of information can be attributed to society itself and not just to the computer, as architectural historian Antoine Picon has noted, citing the findings of James Beniger, Alfred Chandler, and James Cortada: "It was the society of information that made the invention of the computer possible, not the reverse. Some features of digital architecture can be understood only in this extended historical perspective."[20] Yet it is the rapid pace of these changes to which Crary has called attention: "At present, the particular operation and effects of specific new machines or networks are less important than how the rhythms, speeds, and formats of accelerated and intensified consumption are reshaping experience and perception."[21] Regardless of causality, the generation coming to prominence today is unique in that it grew up concurrently with digital technology, which as a result is an integral component of their process. These digital natives are more adaptable to the fundamental shifts in the discipline that occur with each advance in technology—not only the tools that affect how architecture is created but also the outlets through which it is disseminated. The five case studies provide a cross section of emerging practitioners who represent a pluralist approach and whose projects position architecture within historical, technological, and social contexts.

Bureau Spectacular: Jimenez Lai

Jimenez Lai, who founded Bureau Spectacular in Chicago in 2008, is a consumer of architecture. Using overt references as a framework for or an element in his own designs, Lai draws on architectural history and theory, from which he develops a mash-up of ideas and techniques stemming from well-known projects by other practitioners. He appropriates and consumes precedents and reimagines them as a means not only to plot multiple histories of architecture but also to create his own new narratives and interpretations.

Lai relies heavily on a hand-drawn, cartoonish style that he values for its openness to interpretation. For him, drawing by hand, once central to the discipline, can also be used as a discursive device to express ideas. This method has strong ties to the history of the field, for example, in the distinct cartoonlike images by the avant-garde group Archigram (see fig. 14) and in Tigerman's "architoons."[22] Lai has invented his own type of architoon to formulate his theories about architecture. His 2014 collage *Inside Outside Between Beyond* (fig. 15) can easily be compared to Tigerman's *Career Collage* of 1983 (fig. 16) both in style and in the way each architect has presented his theories in the format of a drawing. Tigerman depicted his career using illustrations of all his projects to date and also identified, in a succession of columns at the top of the drawing, the theoretical path from

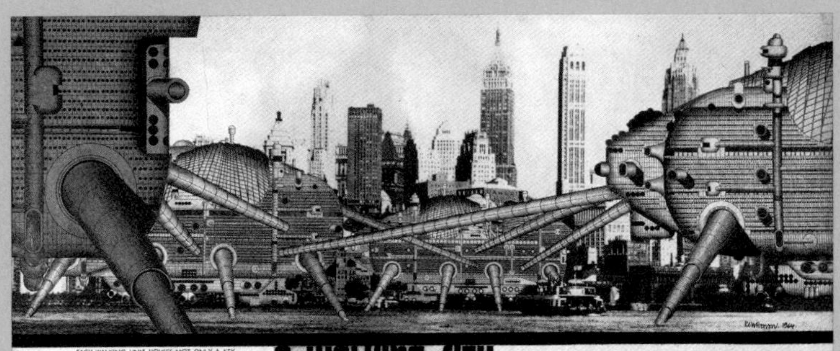

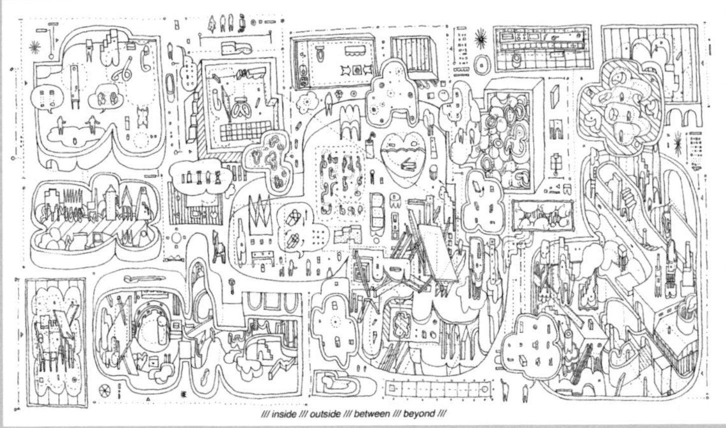

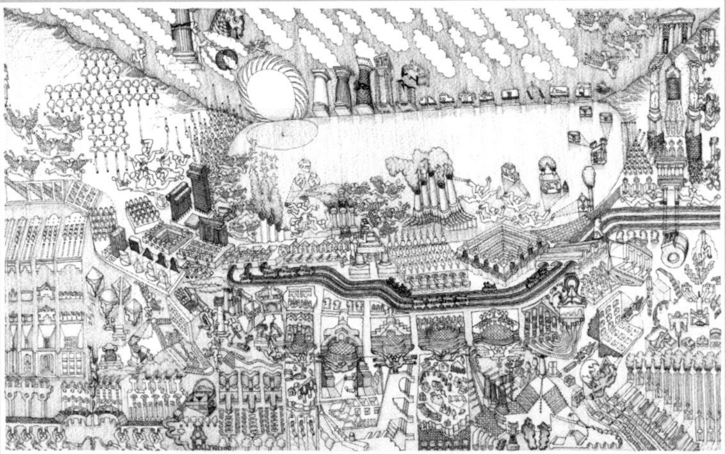

Fig. 14. Archigram / Ron Herron, *The Walking City in New York*, 1964

Fig. 15. Jimenez Lai, *Inside Outside Between Beyond*, 2014

Fig. 16. Stanley Tigerman, *Career Collage*, 1983

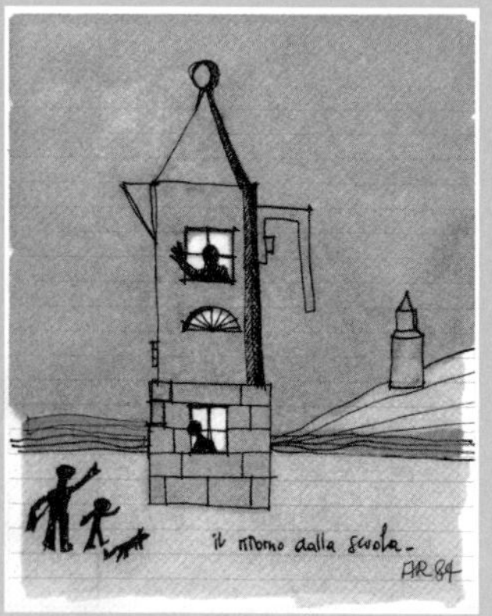

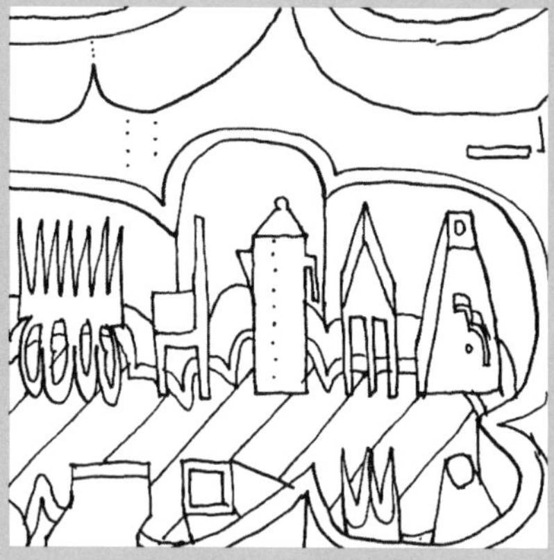

Fig. 17. Aldo Rossi, *Drawing for Espresso Coffeemaker "La cornica": The Return from School*, 1984
Fig. 18. Jimenez Lai, *Inside Outside Between Beyond*, detail of La cornica, 2014

classical architecture to modernism to postmodernism that informed his work. Lai's drawing makes overt reference to projects by other architects who have inspired him, including, for example, Aldo Rossi's teapot (figs. 17, 18), Japanese architectural firm SANAA's Moriyama House (figs. 19, 20), and Lynn's Slavin House (figs. 21, 22). The structure of the work resembles the layout of a comic-book page, yet the ambiguity that Lai has intentionally created raises questions about the conventions of architectural plans and sections while advancing new narratives that branch out from these existing conversations.

Cartoonish Metropolis (2011; pp. 20–21), a drawing of a self-contained city, explores Lai's interest in pareidolia—the way that our minds automatically seek recognizable images. The drawing is intentionally ambiguous so that it can be seen either as a floor plan or as a cross section, depending on how the viewer reads the orientation of the bulbous shapes. As a plan, it depicts compartmentalized rooms, in a clear conversation with floor plans by SANAA for the 21st Century Museum of Contemporary Art in Kanazawa, Japan (1999; fig. 23); as a section, it refers to works such as John Hejduk's Wall House 2 (1973/2001; fig. 24). Furthermore, the fractionalized space anticipates the layout of Lai's *Citizens of No Place: An Architectural Graphic Novel* (2012; fig. 25), in which he articulated, expressly through the format of a graphic novel, his own theories about architectural design, while also exploring the relationship of his ideas to history. It opens with the following statement: "Fiction is the impetus to architecture. Imagination is an upstream process toward making the fake become

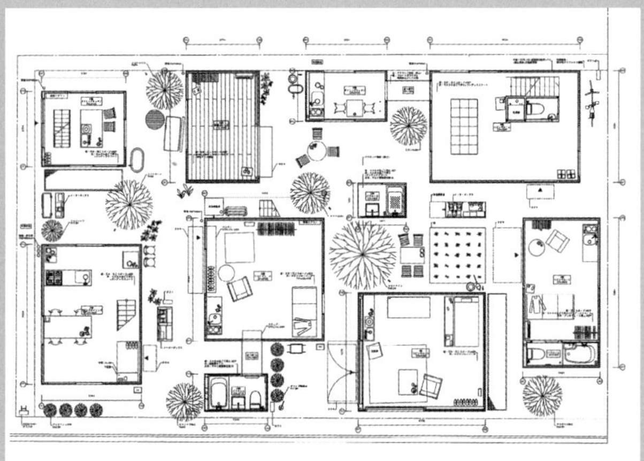

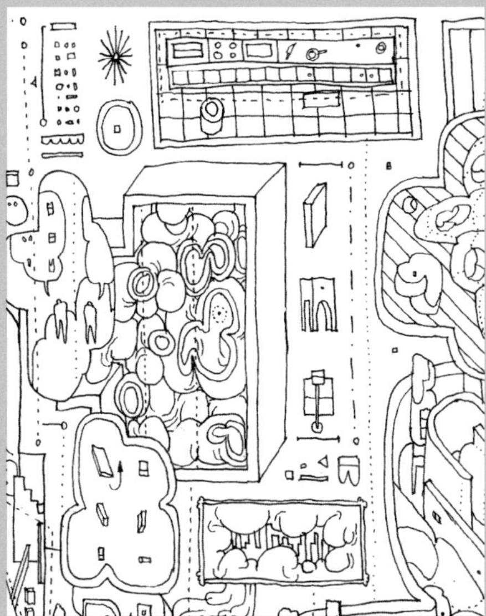

Fig. 19. SANAA / Kazuyo Sejima and Ryue Nishizawa, Moriyama House, Tokyo, Japan, floor plan, 2005

Fig. 20. Jimenez Lai, *Inside Outside Between Beyond*, detail of Moriyama House, 2014

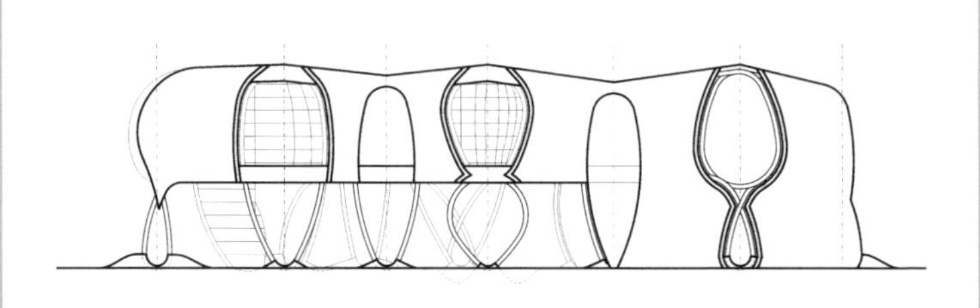

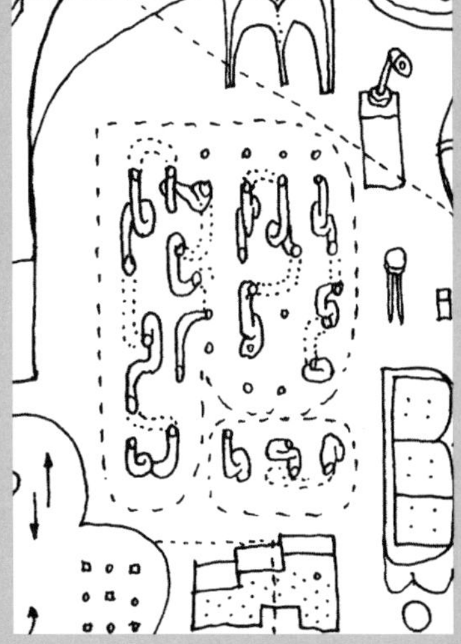

Fig. 21. Greg Lynn, Slavin House, elevation, 2005

Fig. 22. Jimenez Lai, *Inside Outside Between Beyond*, detail of Slavin House, 2014

real. The fiction that architects write—as an inspiration for and response to culture—forecasts the fabrication of cities, which marks history."[23] Further emphasizing Lai's relationship to history, the novel unpacks key issues in architectural theory, including the relationship of the developer to architecture; image, perception, and orientation; the plan versus the cross section; and uniqueness, iconicity, and form. An underlying basis for much of his current work, *Citizens of No Place* details Lai's early thinking about how to use architectural history to craft his own new narrative about the discipline.

More recent works such as *Frankenstein Studies: Stacked Landscapes (MVRDV)* and *Tschumi Transcripts* (both 2014; pp. 17, 22–23) were made with no exact orientation. Similar to *Cartoonish Metropolis* and *Inside Outside Between Beyond*, these drawings are a compilation of theories and precedents collaged together to form new relationships. In *Frankenstein Studies*, Lai combined architecture firm MVRDV's Netherlands Pavilion for Expo 2000 in Hanover (fig. 26)

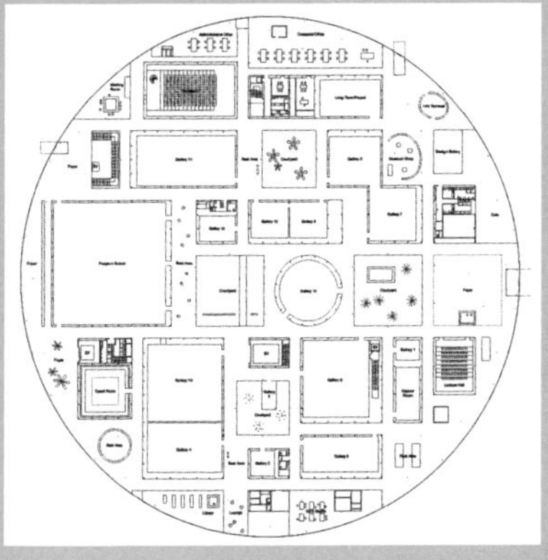

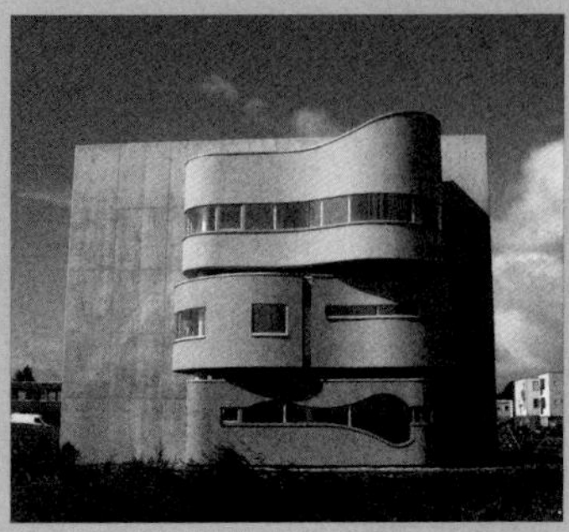

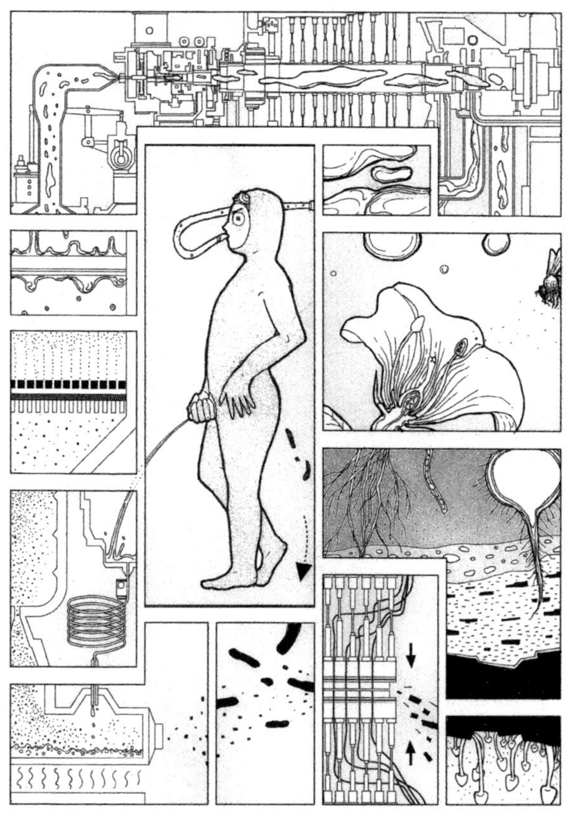

Fig. 23. SANAA / Kazuyo Sejima and Ryue Nishizawa, 21st Century Museum of Contemporary Art, Kanazawa, Japan, floor plan, 1999

Fig. 24. John Hejduk, Wall House 2, Groningen, the Netherlands, designed 1973, built 2001

Fig. 25. Jimenez Lai, *Citizens of No Place: An Architectural Graphic Novel*, page 6, 2012

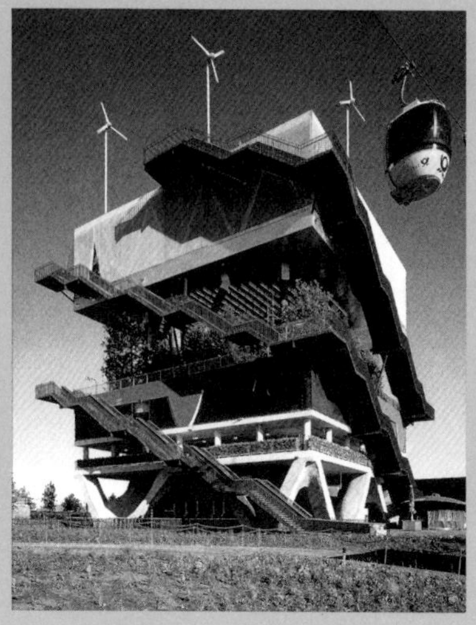

Fig. 26. MVRDV, Netherlands Pavilion, Expo 2000, Hanover, Germany

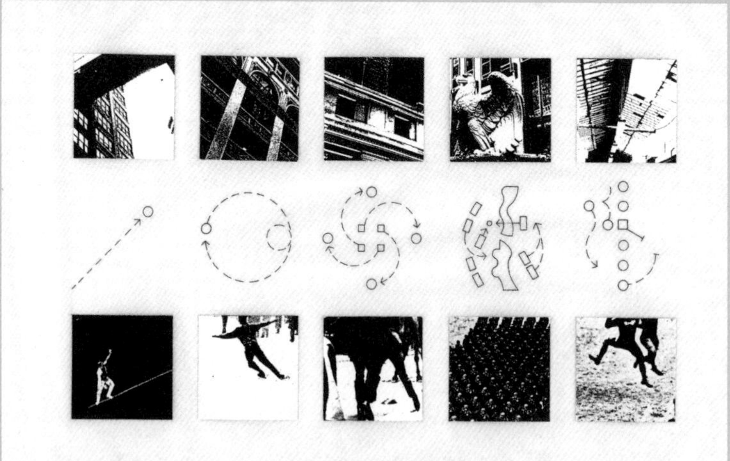

Fig. 27. Bernard Tschumi, *The Manhattan Transcripts Project, Episode 4: The Block*, 1980–81

with Le Corbusier's "Five Points of Modern Architecture,"[24] while *Tschumi Transcripts* is a mash-up of Bernard Tschumi's Manhattan Transcripts (1976–81; fig. 27); both drawings recombine historical elements to create a new architecture—even an architectural world—that could extend from this history. Lai's use of narrative as a tool resonates with the approach of Tschumi, whose Manhattan Transcripts "proposed to transcribe an architectural interpretation of reality."[25] Outlining the value of notation and sequence in fully articulating an

Fake Industries Architectural Agonism

Rooms: No Vacancy, with MAIO, 2014

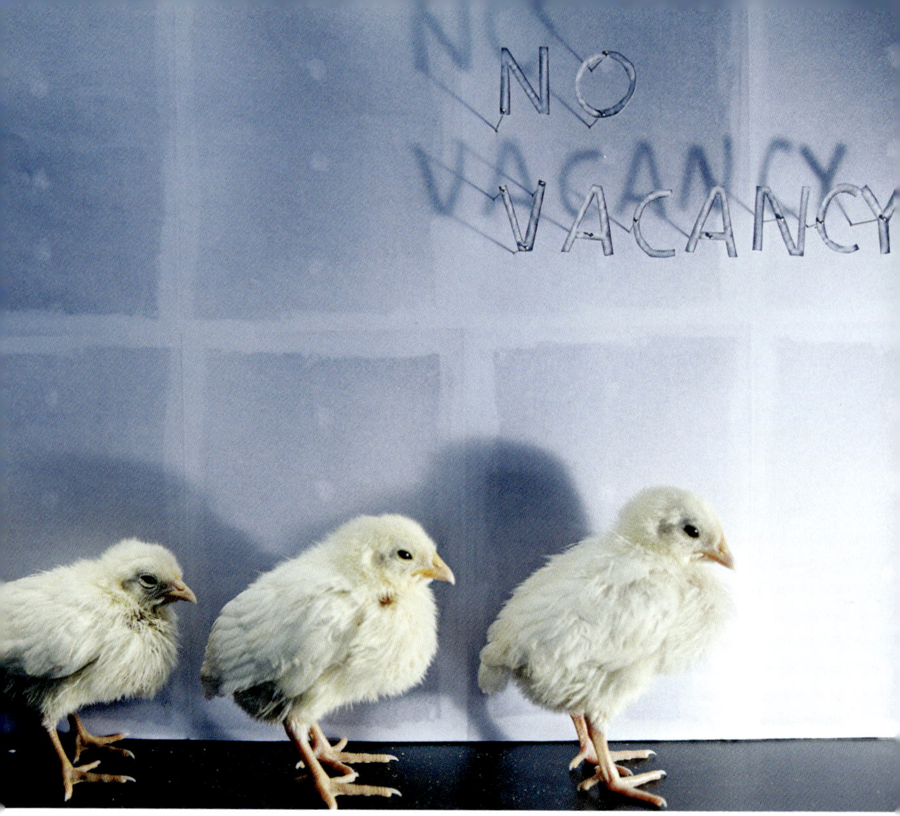

NO
VACANCY

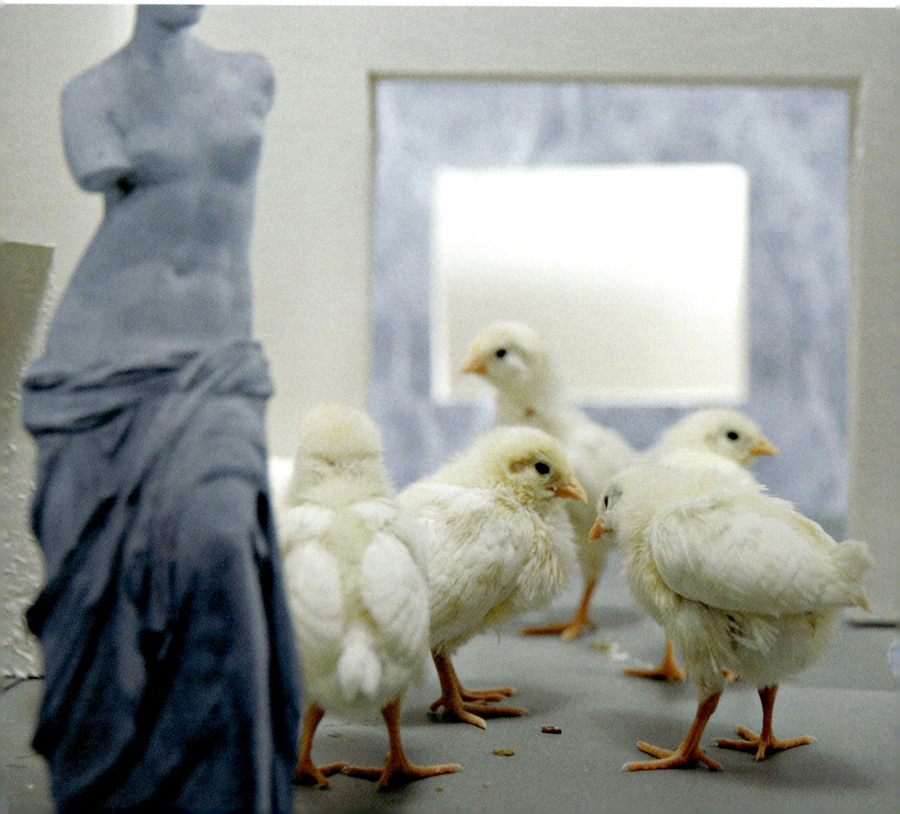

43 ROOMS
A Catalogue

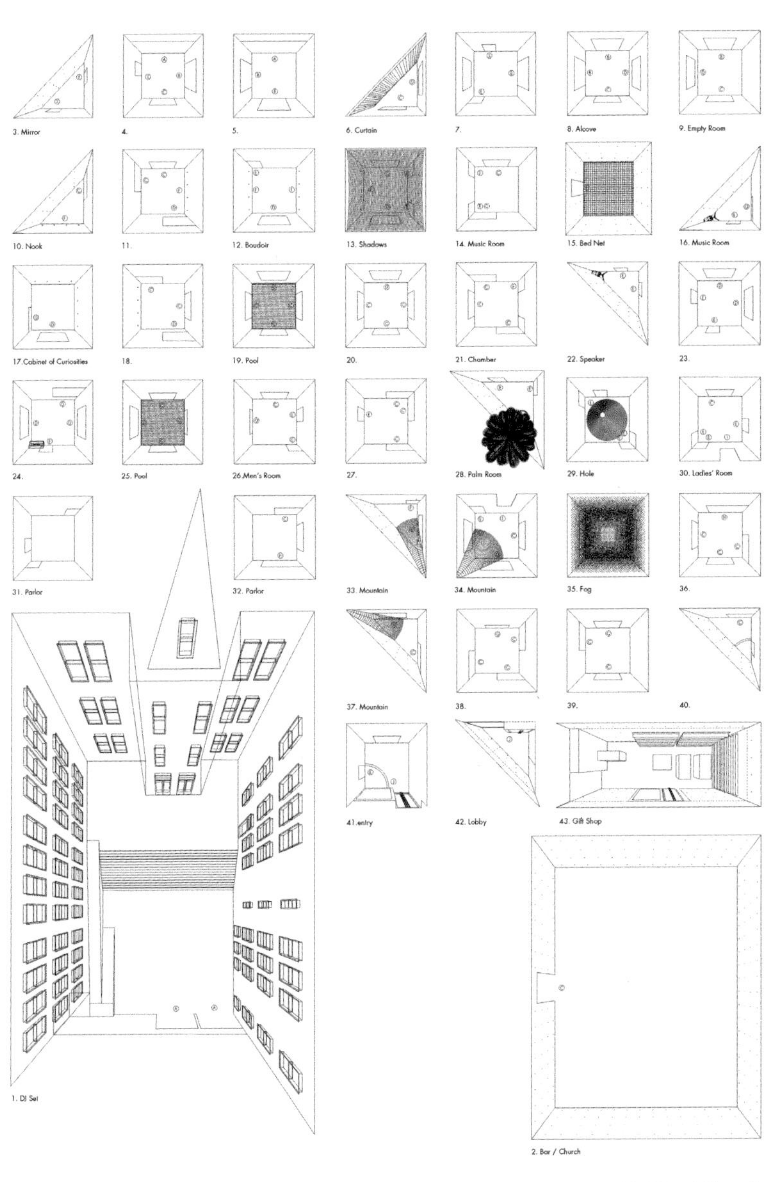

Ⓐ Threshold - 12′ high 16′ wide
Ⓑ Threshold - 12′ high, 8′ wide
Ⓒ Threshold - 8′ high, 8′ wide
Ⓓ Window - 8′ high, 8′wide, 4′ above ground
Ⓔ Threshold - 8′ high, 4′ wide
Ⓕ Holes - 6″ Diameter
Ⓖ Threshold - 4′ high, 8′ Wide
Ⓗ Threshold - 8′ high, 12′ wide
Ⓘ Window - 8′ high, 4′ wide, 8′ above ground
Ⓙ MoMA PS1 Courtyard Front Door

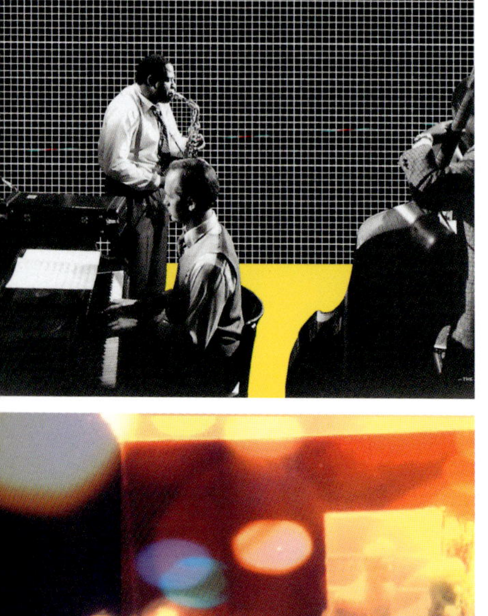
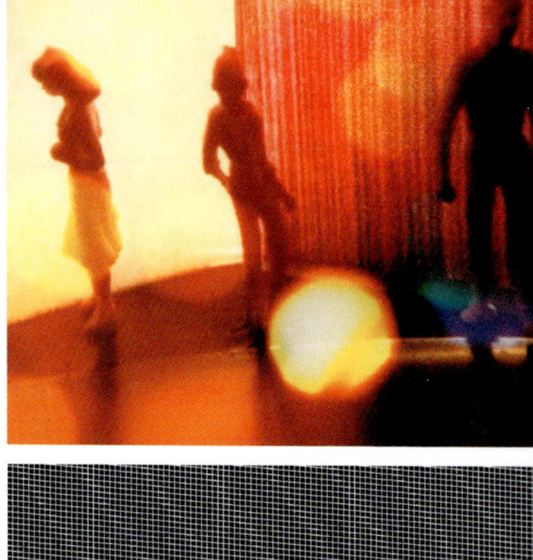

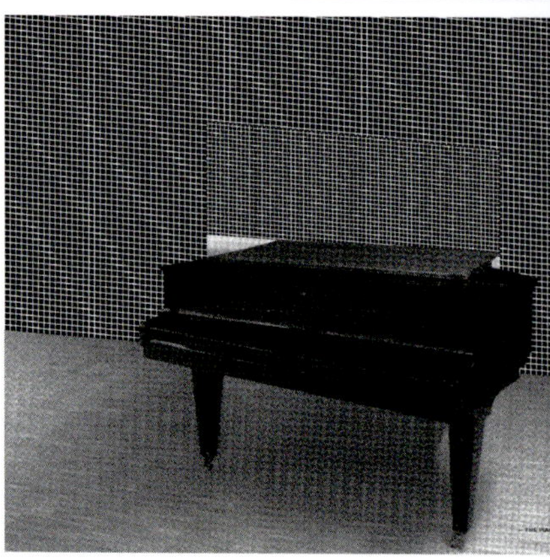
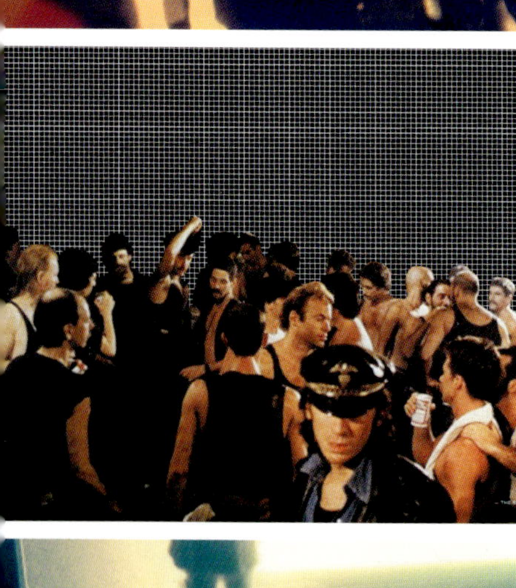
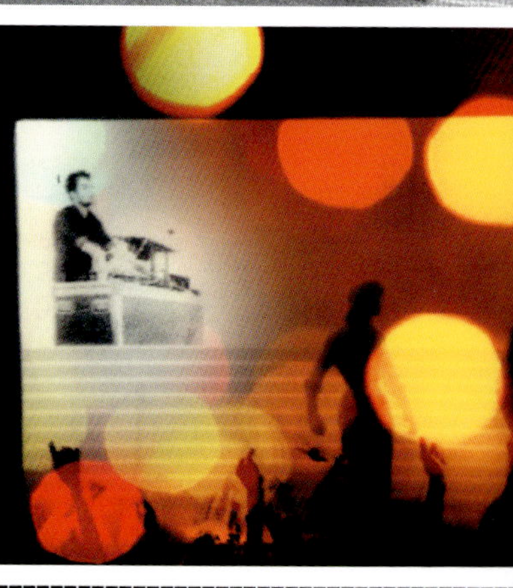
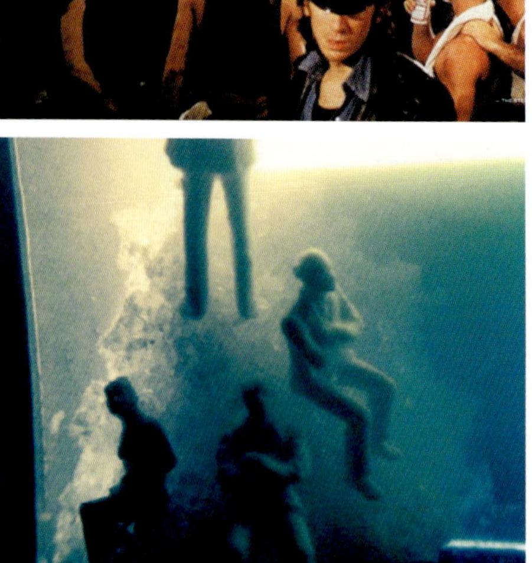
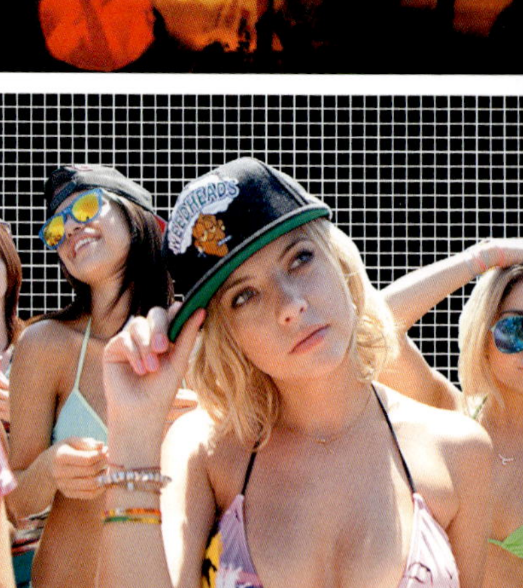

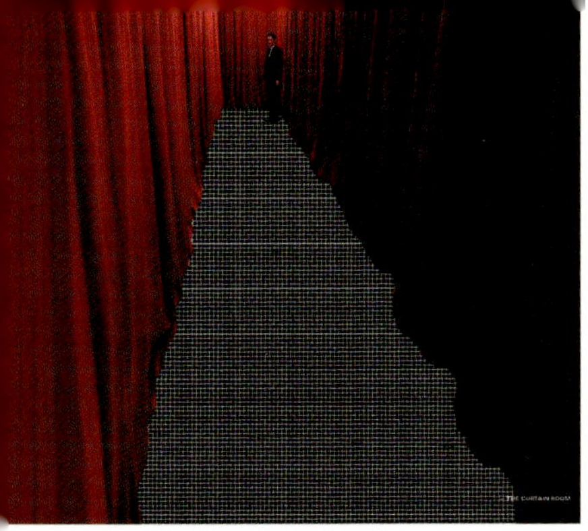

THE CURTAIN ROOM

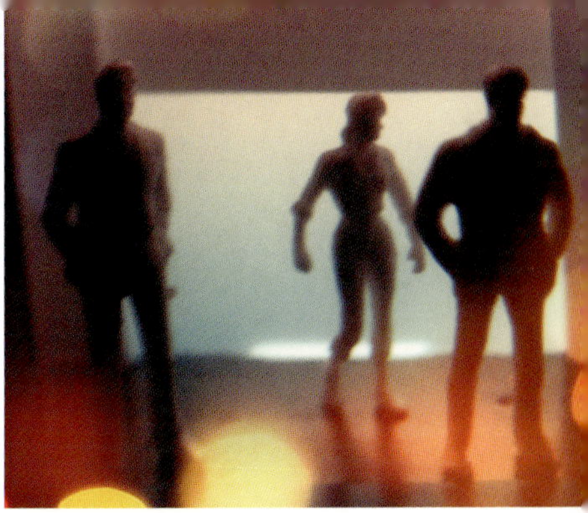

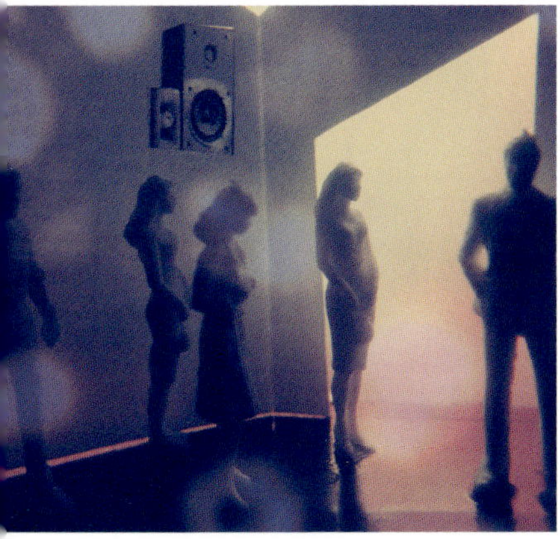

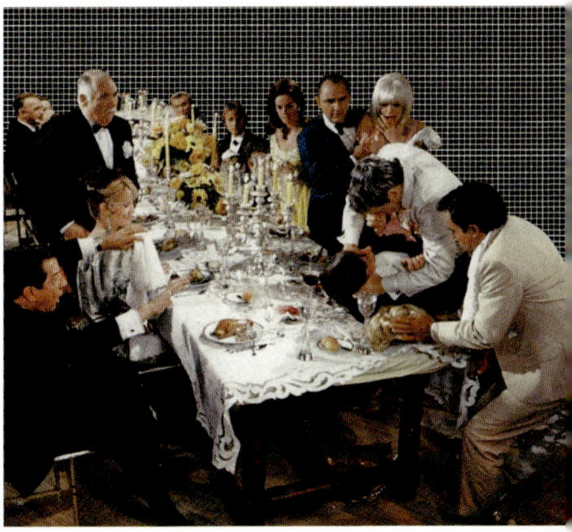

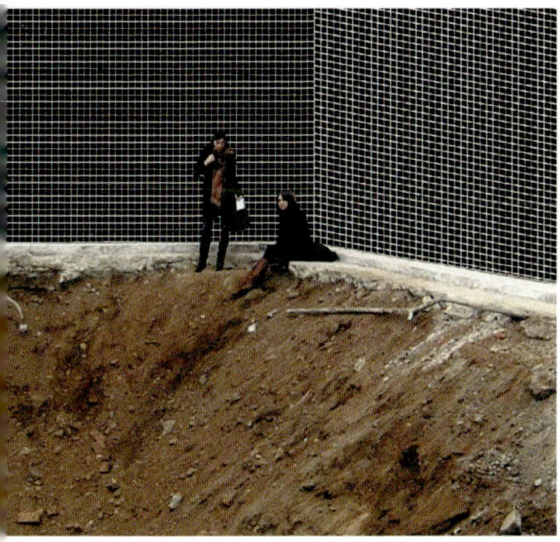

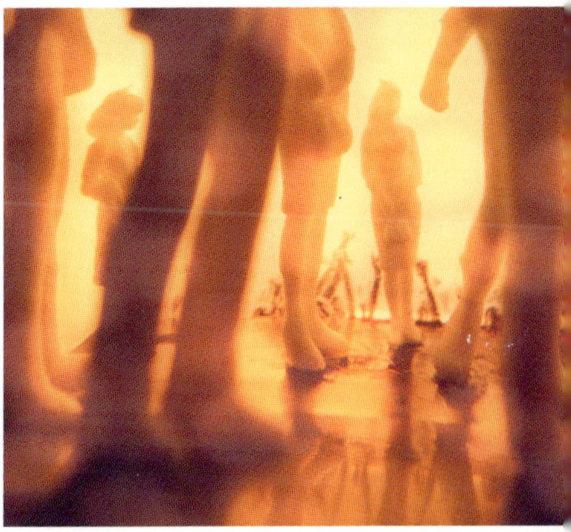

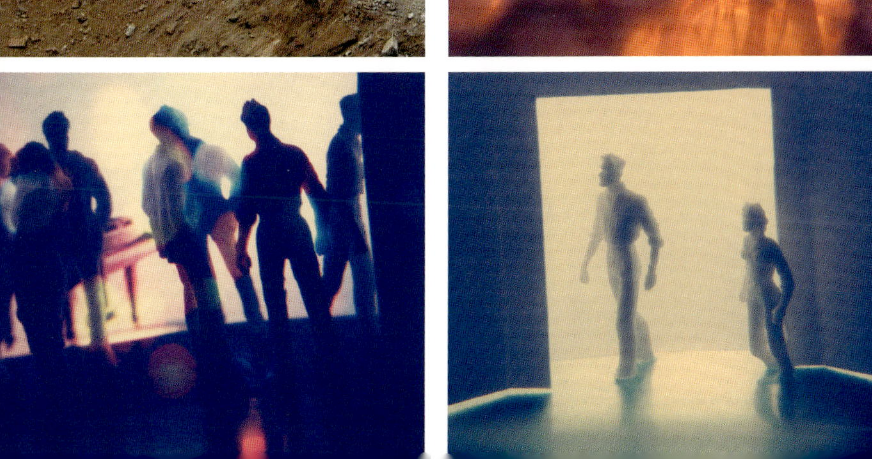

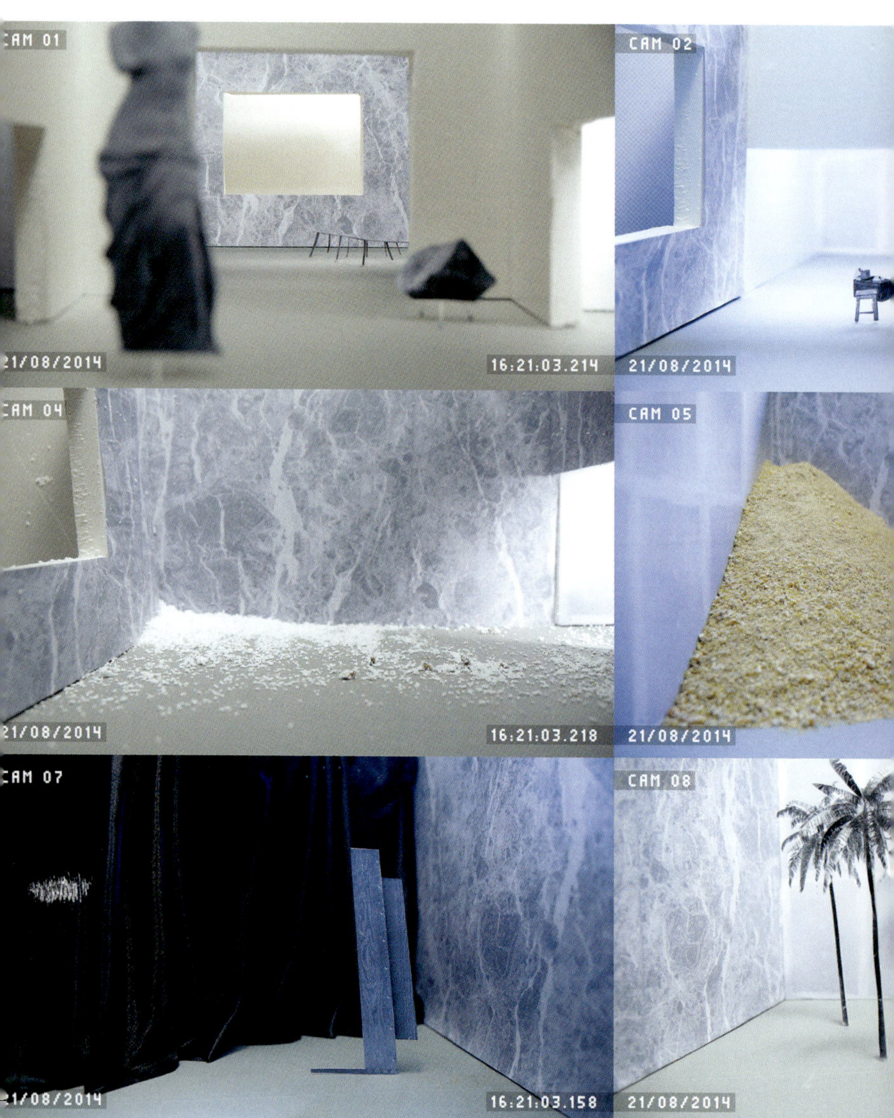

CAM 01
21/08/2014
16:21:03.214
CAM 02
21/08/2014
CAM 04
21/08/2014
16:21:03.218
CAM 05
21/08/2014
CAM 07
21/08/2014
16:21:03.158
CAM 08
21/08/2014

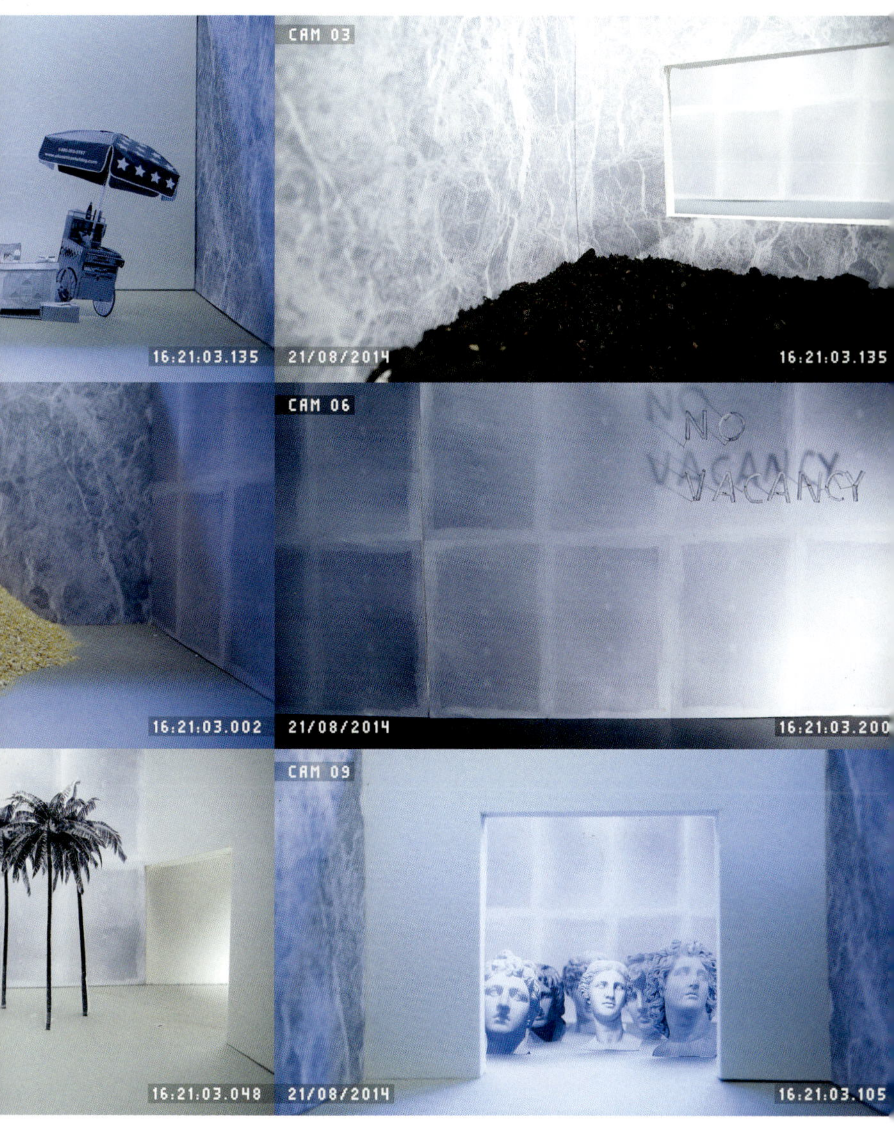

CAM 03
16:21:03.135
21/08/2014
16:21:03.135
CAM 06
NO VACANCY
16:21:03.002
21/08/2014
16:21:03.200
CAM 09
16:21:03.048
21/08/2014
16:21:03.105

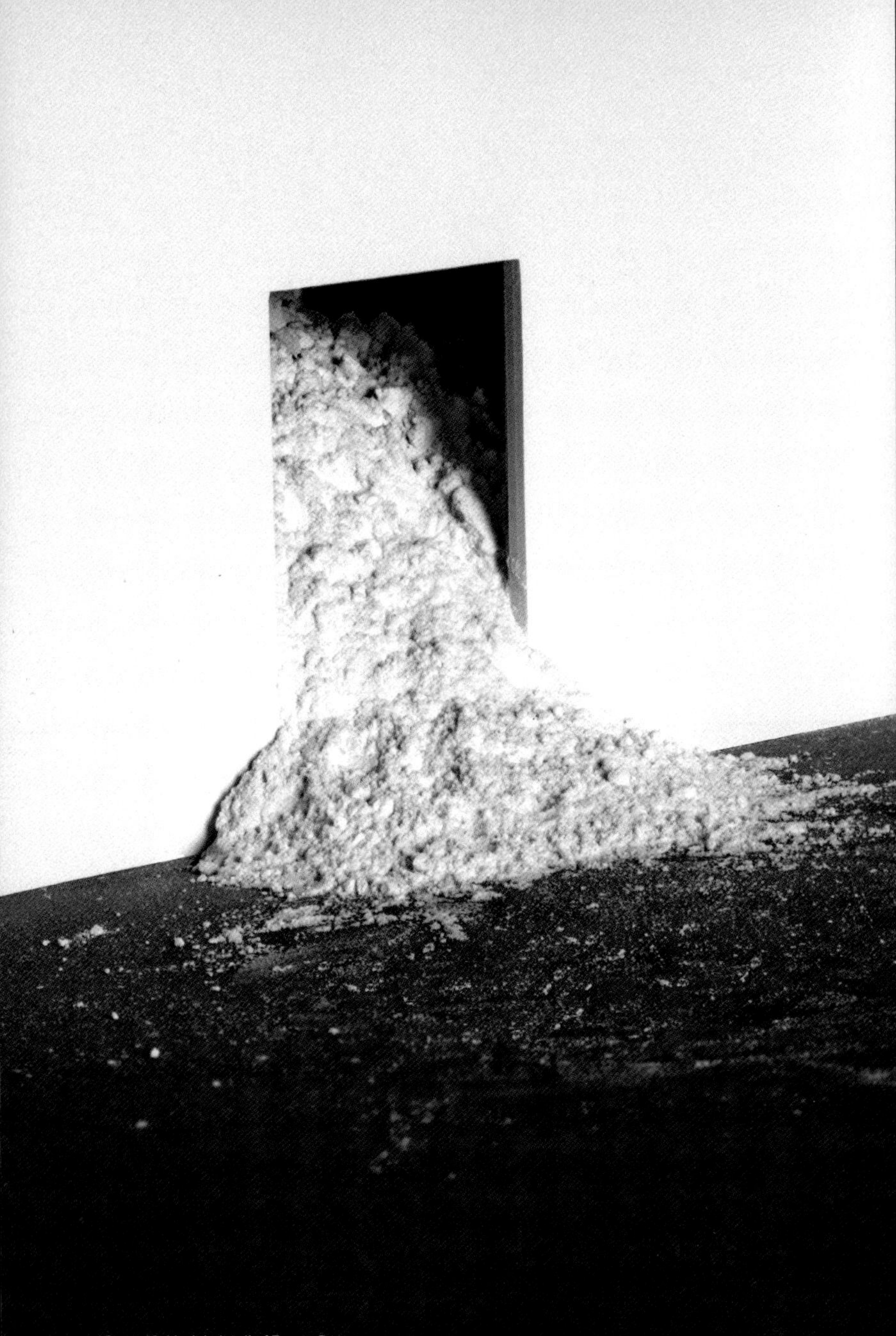

Page 49: Model, detail of Empty Room

Page 50: Video still frames

Page 51: Diagram

Pages 52–53: Details, from left to right: Jam Room collage; Curtain Room model; Curtain Room collage; Empty Room model; Mirror Room model; Piano Room collage; Speakers model; Table Room collage; Steamy Room collage; DJ Set model; Hole Room collage; Fog model; Mountain model; Pool Room collage; Avante-Chambre model; Pool model

Pages 54–55: Video still frames

Page 56: Model, detail of Dune Room

idea, Tschumi observed, "If I define architecture as space occupied by bodies and the motions of bodies in that space, then inevitably I need a vehicle, an instrument, a tool in order to describe the interaction between that space and the movement of the body. So immediately the necessity of introducing a mode of notation becomes apparent. What was new in the Manhattan Transcripts was to introduce it as an essential part of the definition of what architecture is."[26]

Lai's drawings are the conduit for his narratives, and both a starting point and a conceptual foundation for his three-dimensional installations and buildings. With its focus on research and theory, his practice enables him to synthesize information and explore theoretical ideas and architectural opportunities. The way information is embedded in the images of works such as *Cartoonish Metropolis* and *Citizens of No Place* exemplifies what art historian and critic David Joselit has described as "image power—the capacity to format complex and multivalent links through visual means—[which] is derived from networks rather than discrete objects. This means that works of art must develop ways to build networks into their form by, for example, *reframing*, *capturing*, *reiterating*, and *documenting* existing content—all aesthetic procedures that explicitly presume a network as their 'ground.'"[27] It is through such a connective approach, and through his ability to pull unlimitedly from history and from a continuous flow of information, that Lai constructs conversations aimed at opening up new meanings for contemporary architecture.

Formlessfinder: Garrett Ricciardi and Julian Rose

Formlessfinder is an architecture firm in Brooklyn, New York, founded by Garrett Ricciardi and Julian Rose in 2010 on the premise of finding formlessness in architecture. They describe their practice as a methodological laboratory, operating with the goal of freeing architecture from the constraints of form, which has "always served to limit and control." Noting that architectural design has historically been driven by form—from Renaissance ideals of proportion to systems of formal symbols in postmodern architecture—they aim to develop instead a generative type of formlessness, with a mission to "recover architecture's latent possibilities" and "reimagine architecture's future."[28] For Ricciardi and Rose, formlessness is not a disavowal of architecture but stems from their commitment *to* architecture: "We don't want to run away from form or repress it. Our goal is not the paradox of an architecture that never takes shape. We want to change form's role in the discipline, and thereby change the ways in which architecture is conceived, experienced, and understood."[29] Their stance on form is strongly influenced by philosopher Georges Bataille and art historians Yves-Alain Bois and Rosalind Krauss. Bataille's disinterest in architecture was juxtaposed with his affirmation of the formless qualities of space—a potential that Ricciardi and Rose aim to capture through architecture. Their ideas about formlessness as a way that architecture can operate or perform draw from Bois and Krauss's key 1997 publication *Formless: A User's Guide*, in which they declared, "Nothing in and of itself, the formless has only an operational existence: it is a performative, like obscene words, the violence of which derives less from semantics than from the very *act* of their delivery. . . . The formless is an operation."[30] Formlessfinder's motivation is to find the opportunities for action that formlessness can open up in architecture.

In their approach to formlessness, Ricciardi and Rose have created a custom-designed computer application as a methodological aid, an ongoing, open-ended collection of elements that they describe as "part dictionary, part product catalog, part archive, part database, part interactive design tool."[31] Appropriately named the formlessfinder, it is their own repository of chatter. As the two architects gather information—fragments of ideas, architectural theory, historical research and references, material resources, local machinery, and so on—it is entered into the formlessfinder, which they use to research and develop projects. In a world filled with smartphone apps for a range of activities, from navigating the world to doing yoga, they have devised a program with the ability to synthesize information and automate part of the design process.[32] Pairing materials with the logistics of a particular location, for instance, will generate possible strategies and conceptual positions from which to begin a design.

Also embedded within the formlessfinder are critical looks at historical accounts, including a "near misses" category that identifies works in the fields of art and architecture that have bordered on but not quite achieved formlessness. A comparative analysis of philosophical conceptions of form is often a starting point for their projects: for example, the dichotomy between the rigid Platonic cube, which privileges the abstract ideal of form over material, and the

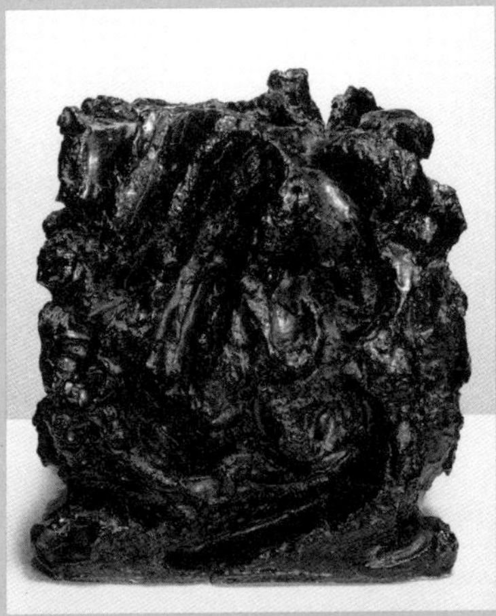

Fig. 28. Lucio Fontana, *Spatial Ceramic*, 1949

Aristotelian emphasis on the inherent properties of material, which allows for a sense of formlessness. Ricciardi and Rose see work such as Lucio Fontana's sculpture *Spatial Ceramic* of 1949 (fig. 28) as a near miss in that it embraces the Aristotelian material qualities of clay even while attempting to conform to Platonic geometry. Greg Lynn's Stranded Sears Tower (p. 32, figs. 11, 12) is also identified as a near miss; his reinterpretation of the Chicago icon comes close, in their view, to achieving formlessness.

The formlessfinder is developed and accessed solely by the firm, and their use of it is distinct for each project and dependent on its specific requirements, location, and budget. In their Tent Pile Pavilion for Design Miami 2013 (pp. 33–40), for example, the location and local materials drove their search for the formless. Recognizing that sand is a natural resource abundant in South Florida, Ricciardi and Rose began to look at the inherent structural properties and possibilities of that material. The confluence of the temporary nature of the project (a five-day international design fair) and local resources of material and machinery led them to a solution in which the formless was manifest as a pile of sand that composed the primary structural support of the cantilevered roof of the pavilion. The sand also provided an opportunity for visitors to engage with the architecture, with many climbing up and lying on the pile. Notably, the design was sustainable: the sand was sourced from Miami's approved supplier and, after the fair was over, it was donated to the city, minimizing waste.[33] When analyzing Tent Pile, Ricciardi and Rose drew a surprising

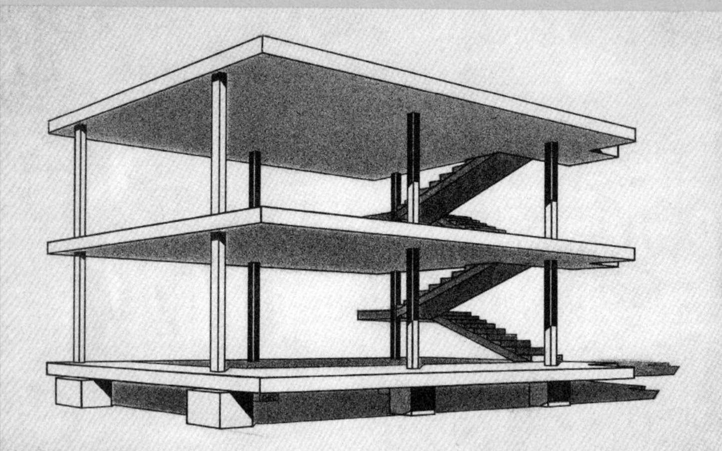

Fig. 29. Le Corbusier, Dom-ino House, 1914–15

analogy between that project and Le Corbusier's Dom-ino House, created between 1914 and 1915 (fig. 29), in that the structures of both comprise the vertical and the horizontal. In Tent Pile, this duality is the result of the way sand operates when piled up, whereas in the Dom-ino House—a prototypical design for a mass-produced home with an open floor plan—two distinct horizontal planes are connected vertically by a staircase. This conceptual linking of two very different types of projects underlines a theoretical premise of their philosophy: that structure can take any form (or formlessness).

While the work of Formlessfinder draws from and relies heavily on history, their method is indebted to and embedded in contemporary ways of thinking and synthesizing information. Overall, their goal is to get away from a prescribed shape, style, or form and to let the inherent qualities of materials and context drive the solution to each project. Their unconventional strategy is an apt expression of Bois and Krauss's declaration, "Thus the dream of architecture, among other things, is to escape entropy."[34]

Fake Industries Architectural Agonism: Cristina Goberna and Urtzi Grau

Founded in 2005 by Cristina Goberna and Urtzi Grau, Fake Industries Architectural Agonism is a nontraditional firm taking a critical stance toward the basic tenets of architectural practice. Their open approach is apparent in the way they divide their operation between New York City, Barcelona, and Sydney, and how they devise distinct collaborations for each project rather than employing a fixed staff, which allows for both flexibility and specificity. Fake Industries is driven by the belief that "the world is full of architecture, more or less interesting; we do not wish to add any more. . . . Don't ask us for new stuff, we copy."[35] For them, architecture is an opportunity to reconceptualize fragments of information and construct new relationships among these data. This notion of copying can be traced back to artists such as Sherrie Levine, who began to borrow from the work of well-known artists in the late 1970s, re-presenting or re-creating it as her own (see fig. 30). Levine's appropriations were identified by artist and critic Jeanne Silverthorne as constituting "a question about the meanings of the past—as well as a critical one, about the values of art in the present."[36] Like Levine, Goberna and Grau are critical of history yet find value in engaging with it, using appropriation as a way to build from and expand ideas. As the *agonism* in their name suggests, their struggle with history is a respectful one, with the aims of creating a new, harmonious balance and forging a worthwhile relationship with the built-in opposition. Their copies are not always overt references to particular architectural precedents, but rather pull from a vast array of influences. Harking back to Joselit's notion of image power, Fake Industries' unique contribution lies in the way they compile, reinterpret, and present bits of information to communicate a new idea.

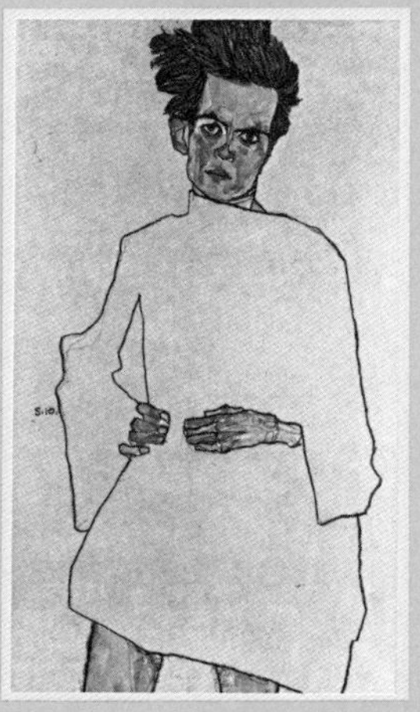

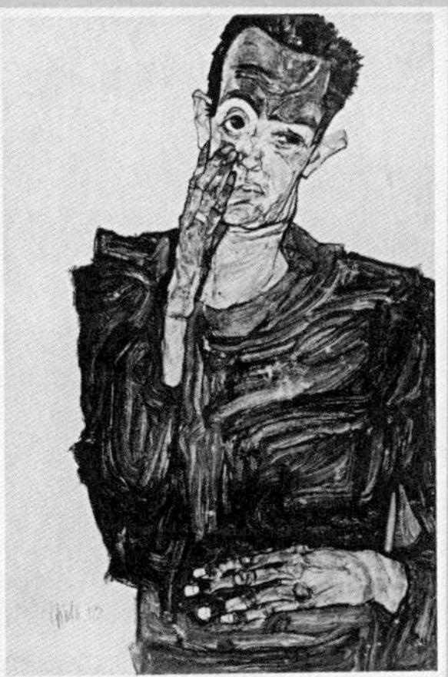

Fig. 30. Sherrie Levine, *After Egon Schiele*, details, 1982

This is illustrated in Rooms: No Vacancy (pp. 49–56), a project that exemplifies their mission. When shortlisted as finalists for the 2014 Museum of Modern Art and MoMA PS1 Young Architects Program, Fake Industries developed a collaboration with Spanish architecture firm MAIO to create their proposal. They began by exploring the history of parties and raves in New York City in venues ranging from the Factory to CBGB to the Mudd Club. Their research revealed three elements essential to the activation of a party: architecture as an enclosure, atmosphere to produce an environment, and human interaction as a catalyst. In analyzing previous PS1 pavilions, Goberna and Grau found that most had existed as objects—which they defined as passive architecture—in the center of the courtyard, without much opportunity for interaction. They were interested in an installation that would facilitate atmospheric conditions and provide enclosures for groups or couples. Stemming from the original mission of PS1—an alternative museum with a series of rooms, each for a site-specific artwork—their design for the pavilion consisted of forty-three individual rooms, each providing a unique, fragmented experience from elements such as "recyclable walls . . . secret entrances . . . windows or holes"; within this framework they planned special rooms to add an element of surprise, such as "the Music Room, the Fog, the Bed Net, the Chamber, etc."[37] By harnessing multiplicity, Fake Industries astutely responded to contemporary trends of identity and publicity, in which projects are largely known by images disseminated via social media. Together, these disparate spaces—and the vast array of unique images of them—built an overall understanding of the pavilion without any prescribed sequence.

Further reflecting our image-based society, in the presentation of their design the firm developed a series of images in varying styles. Each series shows aspects of the individual rooms through atypical views in order to indicate the unique environments of each space, a style that parallels the way Instagram photos work—each one is individual, yet the aggregation of images from multiple perspectives leads to a more comprehensive view of the subject. These images are not devoid of history, and in fact they make direct references to the collage techniques used by Italian architects Archizoom (see fig. 31) and Superstudio (see fig. 32).[38] Goberna and Grau use the same method of fragmentation and compiling history in their presentation video—a sequence of separate shots of numerous rooms and

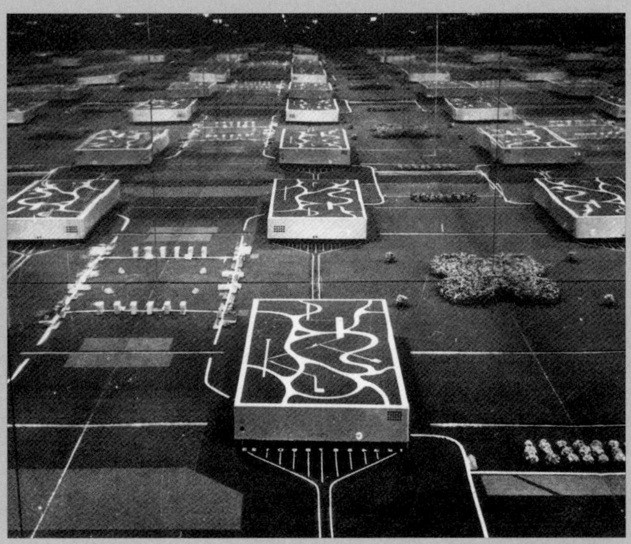

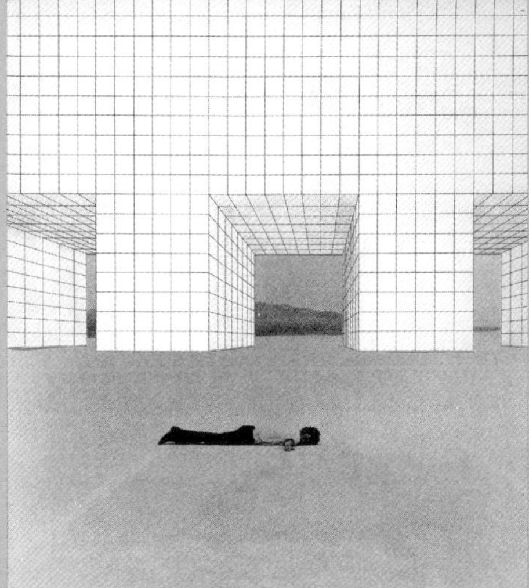

Fig. 31. Design Archizoom Associati, No-Stop City, 1970

Fig. 32. Superstudio / Gian Piero Frassinelli, *The Continuous Monument: With de Maria*, c. 1969

conditions. In each shot, live baby chickens stand in for visitors to the pavilion, experiencing the different material and atmospheric qualities of the rooms. The walls of the model in this video consist of exposed, mudded-and-taped drywall and faux-onyx wallpaper—inexpensive and readily available materials with which the architects proposed to construct the pavilion. The exposed drywall recalls Rem Koolhaas's 2003 design for the Illinois Institute of Technology's

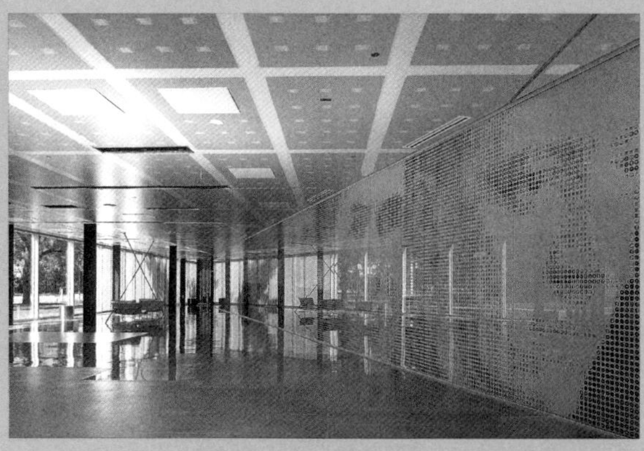

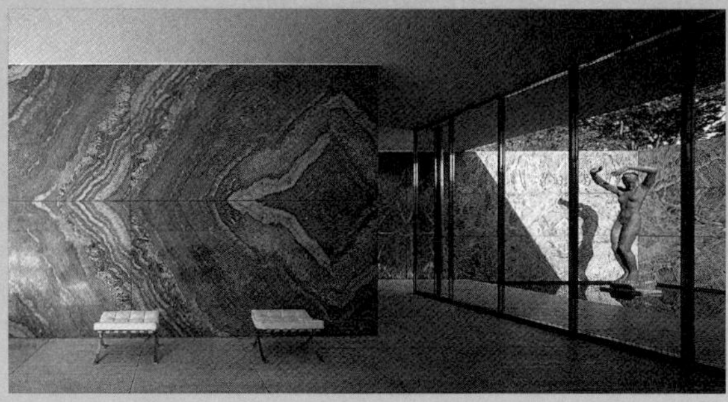

Fig. 33. Office for Metropolitan Architecture / Rem Koolhaas, Illinois Institute of Technology, McCormick Tribune Campus Center, detail of exposed drywall, built 2003

Fig. 34. Ludwig Mies van der Rohe, German Pavilion for the Barcelona Exposition, built 1929, reconstructed 1983–86

McCormick Tribune Campus Center in Chicago (fig. 33) as well as his theory of junkspace, articulated in his response to the surrounding campus—designed by Ludwig Mies van der Rohe—and to modern architecture more broadly.[39] For Koolhaas, "junkspace is what remains after modernization has run its course or, more precisely, what coagulates while modernization is in progress."[40] In the same vein as the mission of Fake Industries, Koolhaas continued, "Junkspace is authorless, yet surprisingly authoritarian."[41] The onyx wallpaper refers to Mies's Barcelona Pavilion, an iconic structure that has transcended time (fig. 34); first built as the German Pavilion at the Barcelona International Exposition in 1929 and then disassembled in 1930, it exists primarily in memory and in images of its 1983–86 reconstruction. Fake Industries, by proposing this inexpensive, paper replication of onyx, further perpetuates Koolhaas's notion of junkspace and his reaction to Mies.

Erin Besler

Low Fidelity, 2012

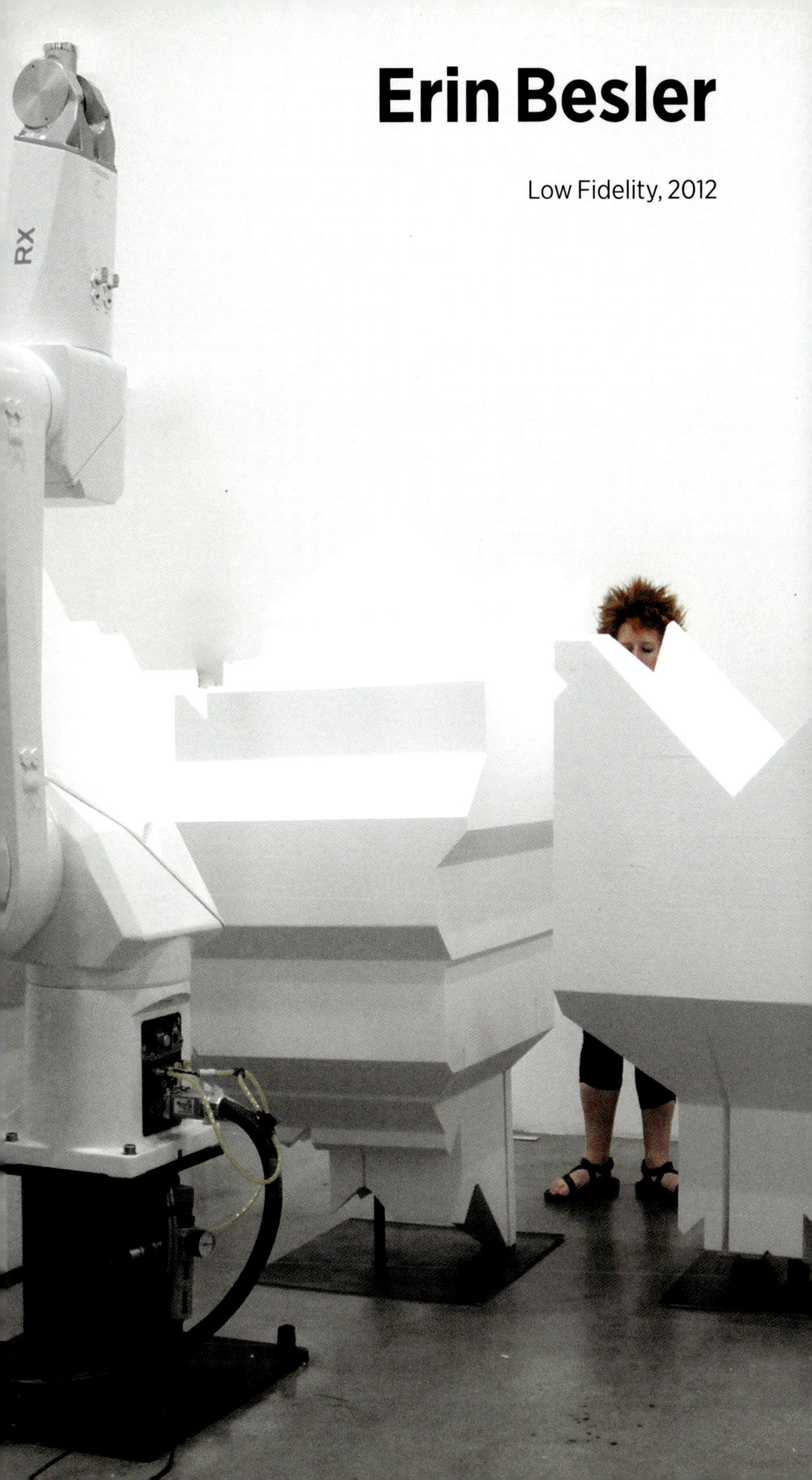

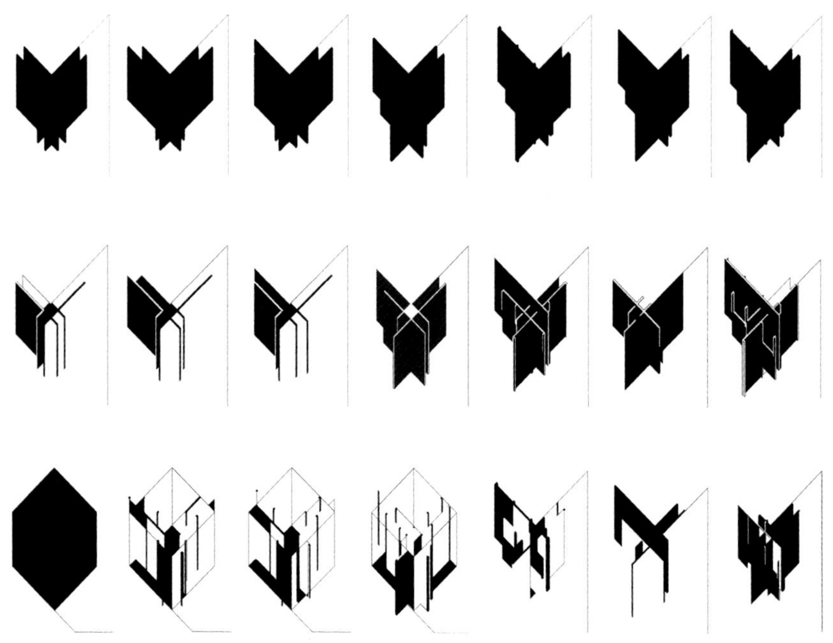

Tool paths produced from Peter Eisenman's fourteen House VI transformations, for the object (top row), the black space (middle row), and the white space (bottom row)

Preceding page: Robot-produced, large-scale foam object-projections for Low Fidelity with Erin Besler and a robot, in the Robot House at the Southern California Institute of Architecture, 2012

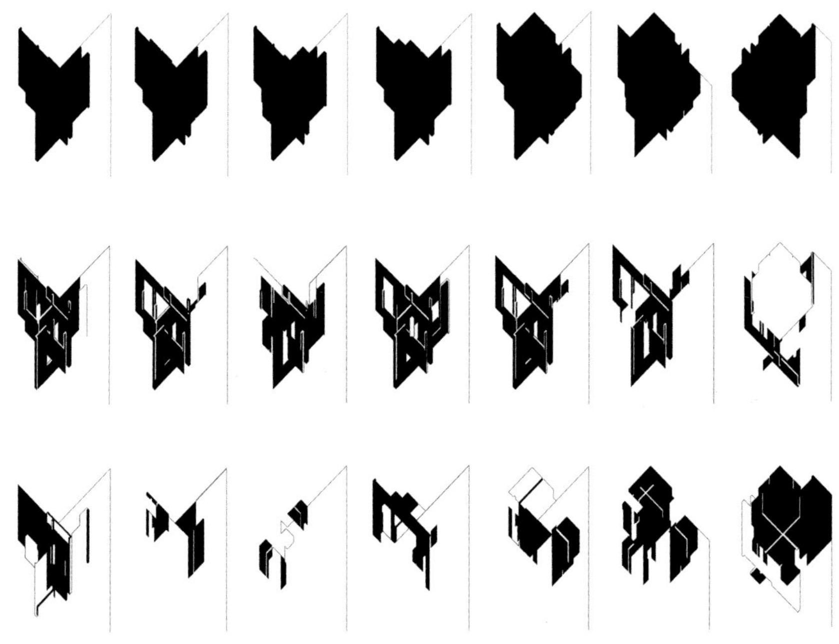

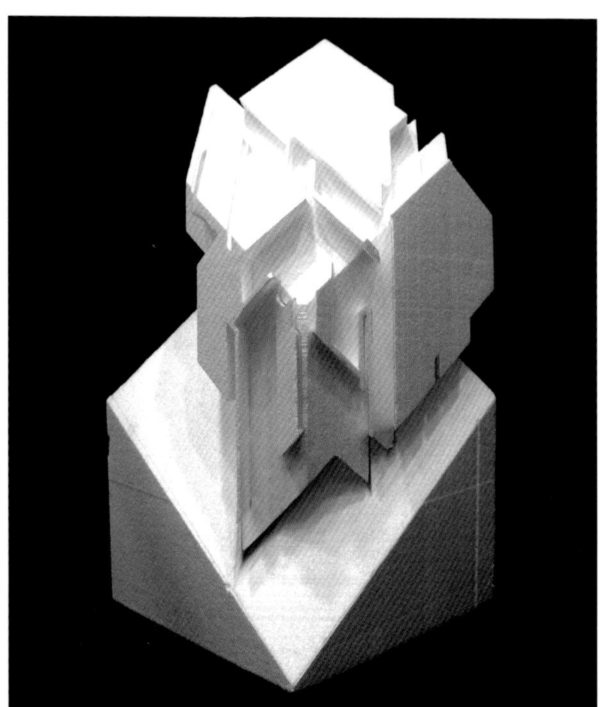

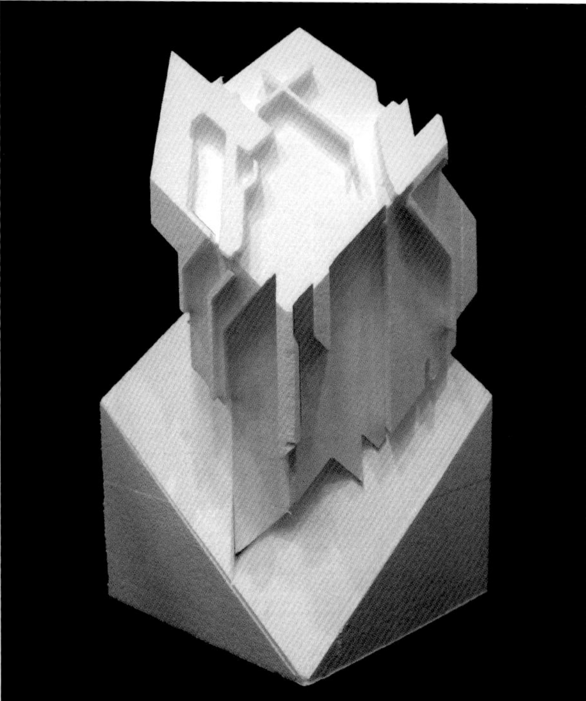

Robot-produced foam object-projections of the black space (top) and the white space (bottom) of the thirteenth transformation

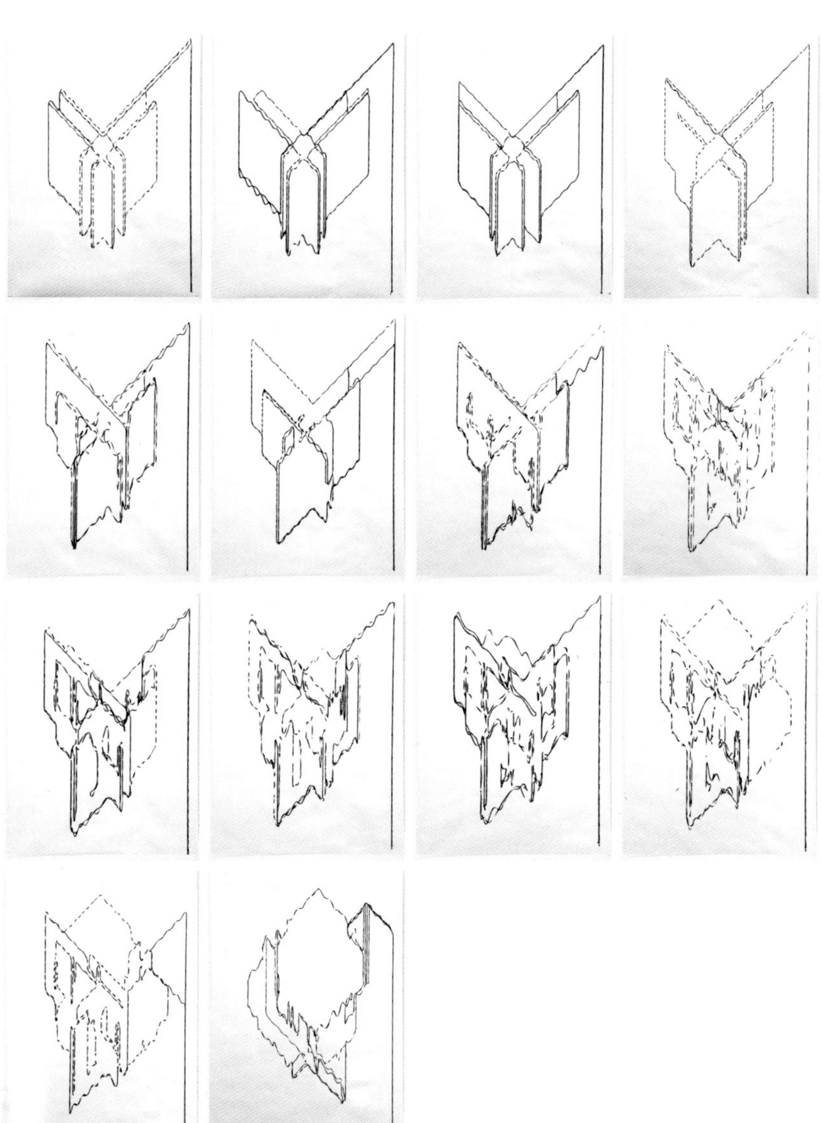

Robot-drawn translations of the black space of the fourteen transformations at 100 percent speed

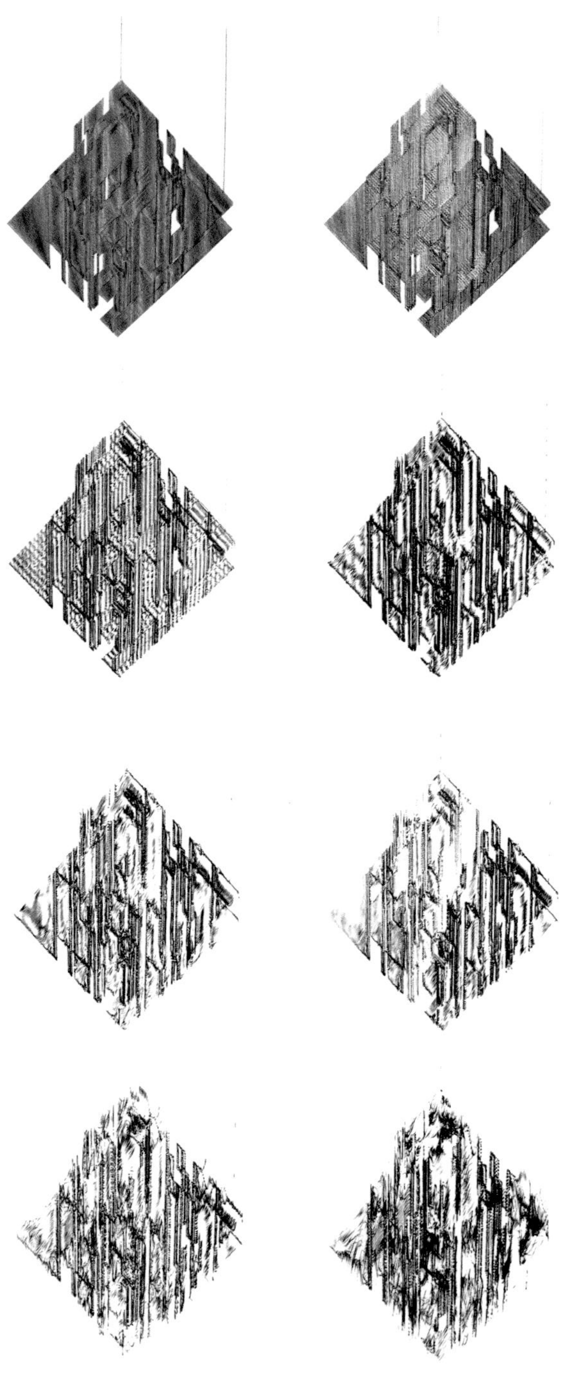

Robot-drawn plans of foam object-projections of the white space of the thirteenth transformation, at speeds of (left to right, from upper-left corner) 1, 2, 5, 10, 25, 50, 75, and 100 percent

Opposite: Details of the robot-drawn plans shown above at speeds of (left to right, from upper-left corner) 1, 5, 25, and 75 percent

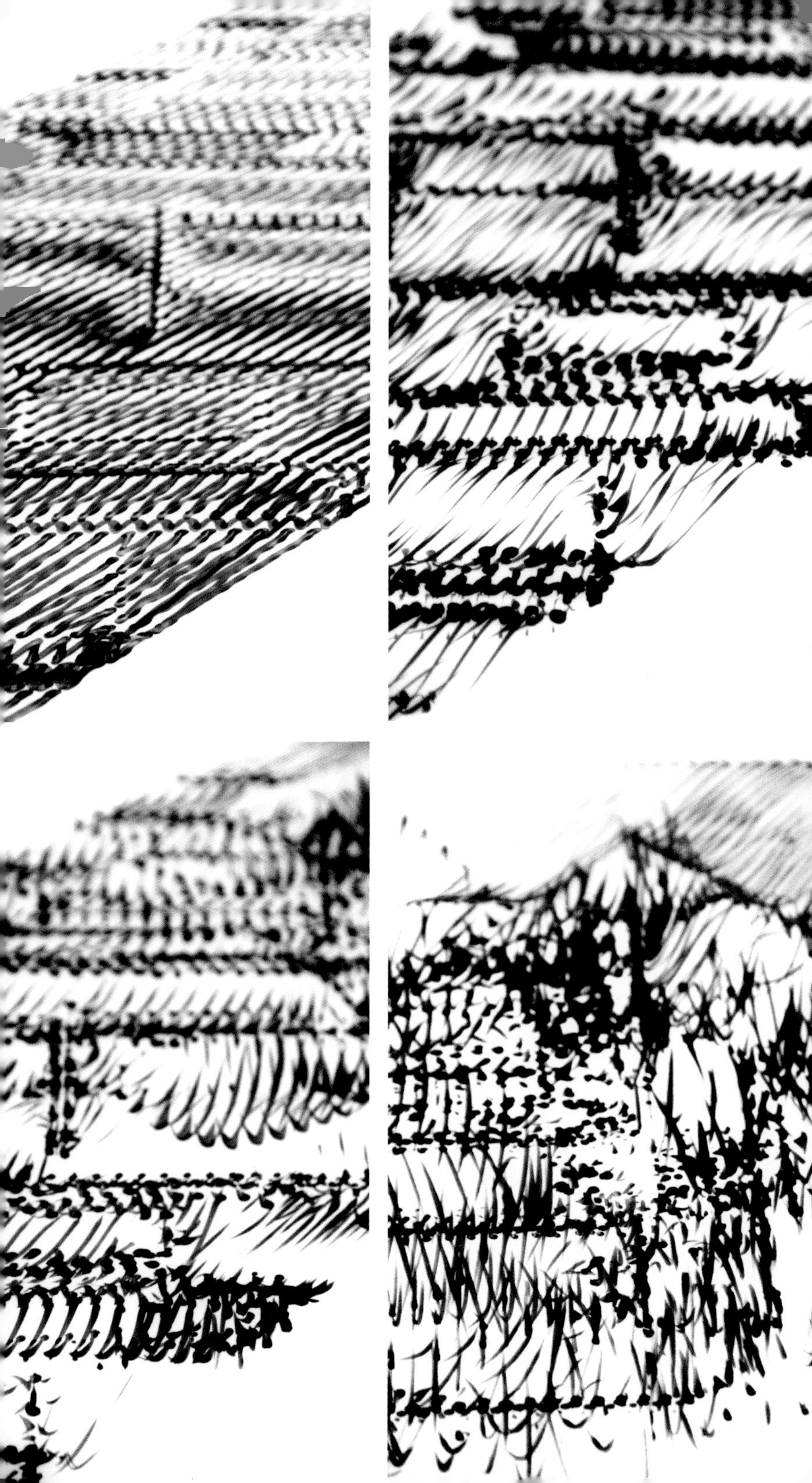

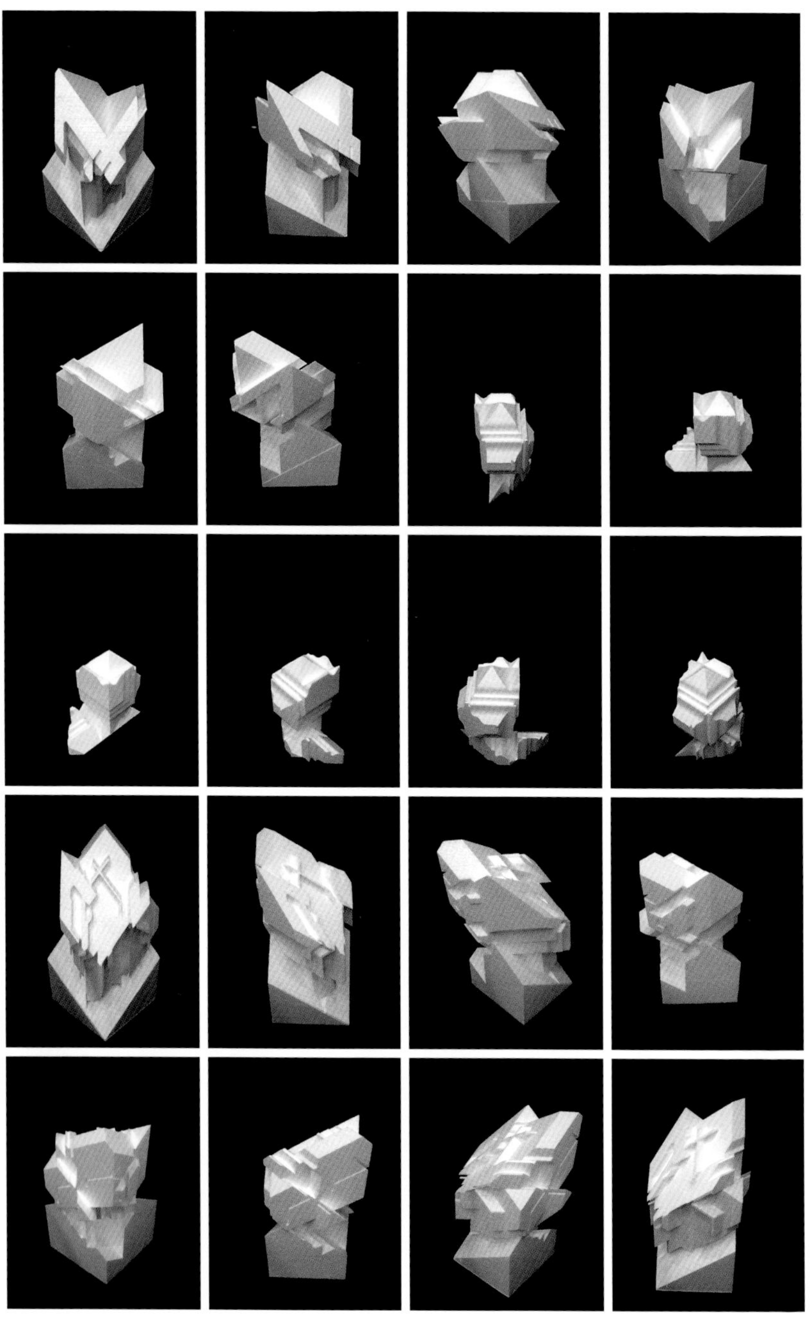

Foam object-projections. Left to right, from upper-left corner, the first six objects are from the black space of the fifth transformation, 36 inches high; the second six objects are from the overall form of the thirteenth transformation, 18 inches high; the last eight objects are from the white space of the thirteenth transformation, 36 inches high

Fake Industries' presentation never provides an overall view of the project; instead, a multitude of individual images reveal different types of conditions and details within the whole. This approach, one that mirrors the way their proposed pavilion would be experienced—as discrete encounters with no set path or sequence—also consciously parallels the way people interface with social media and other contemporary forms of communication.

Erin Besler

Issues surrounding representation have been embedded in architecture throughout the discipline's history, including the translation of ideas into more concrete forms such as drawings and buildings, and, more recently, the influence of emerging technologies. The transition from drawing to object is not always direct; often the drawing represents conceptual, rather than practical, aspects of a project. As architect and historian Robin Evans articulated in his insightful essay "Translations from Drawing to Building," architectural drawings can be discursive: "All things with conceptual dimension are like language, as all grey things are like elephants. A great deal in architecture may be language-like without being language."[42] As the computer introduced new possibilities for creating realistic renderings and videos to simulate an architectural idea, it also allowed for serial and immediate reproduction, thus amplifying issues of translation.

Erin Besler's 2012 thesis project, Low Fidelity (pp. 65–72), explores the relationship of technology to issues in architectural representation, reproduction, and the agency of drawing. While Besler was working on her master's degree at the Southern California Institute of Architecture under the guidance of Andrew Atwood, the school acquired several large robots for the students to use in their studios—machines not widely employed in the profession of architecture. Questioning the immediate acceptance of this technology in a pedagogical context, Besler approached her project with a critical lens. Low Fidelity takes the fourteen published transformations for Peter Eisenman's House VI (1972–75; fig. 35) as its starting point. Besler selected Eisenman and this particular project for several reasons. As one of the early digital architects, he has addressed issues that interest her: multiplicity, seriality, the role of projection as a form of representation and production, and the history and influence of digital

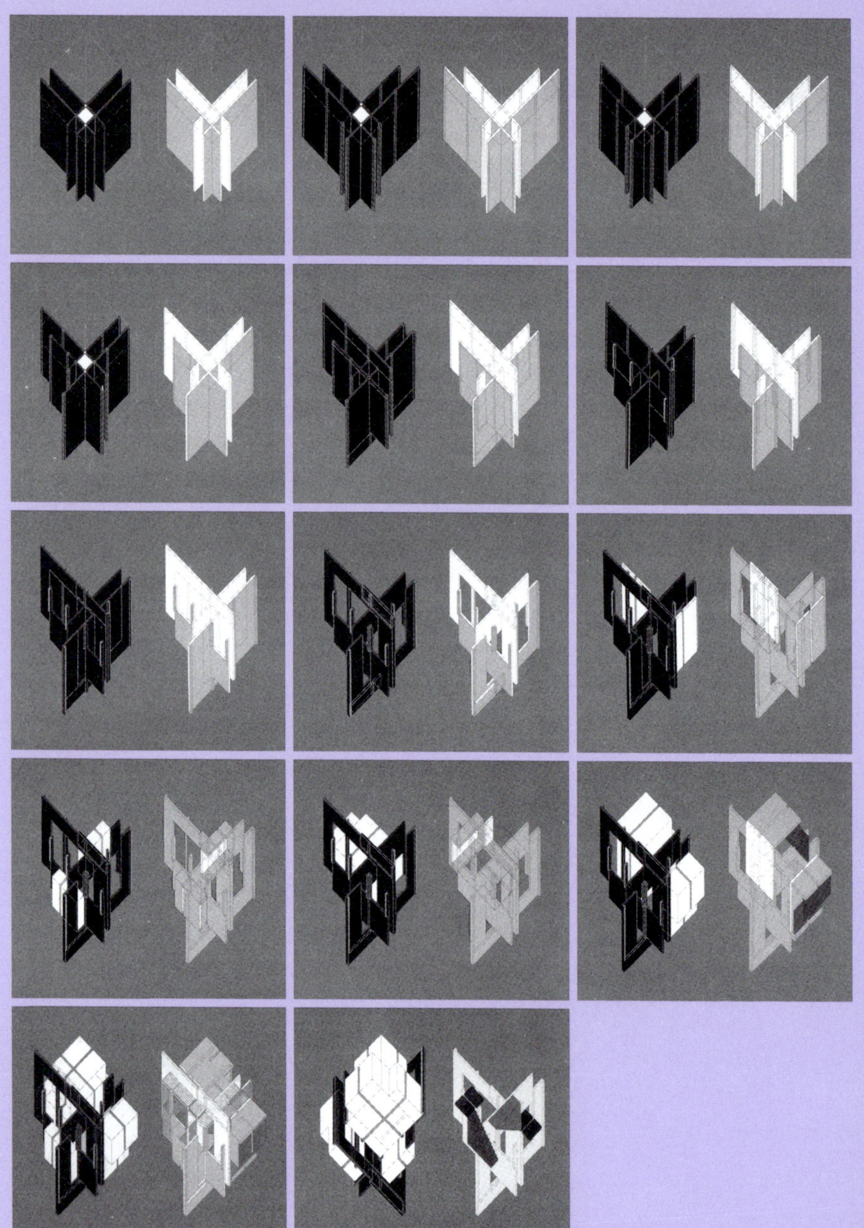

Fig. 35. Peter Eisenman, House VI, Cornwall, Connecticut, Fourteen Transformations (axonometric), 1972–75

technologies in architecture. She was also drawn to the material quality of the House VI transformations. Made from layers of colored paper, they are neither true two-dimensional drawings nor easily identifiable as three-dimensional objects. Eisenman's pieces are part of a lineage of work exploring representation in architecture that he has traced back to the sixteenth century and Italian Renaissance architect Filippo Brunelleschi's invention of one-point perspective.[43] As architecture critic Jeffrey Kipnis described Eisenman's project, "He proposed that one could detach design from the mind-numbing convention of service and, instead, transform a finite set of elements according to generative rules."[44] Applying the same method to Low Fidelity, Besler imposed her own set of generative rules, focusing on the conceptual gaps between Eisenman's layers of paper.

As the basis of her conversation with the field of architecture, Besler took Eisenman's fourteen transformations and dissected each of them into three different types—the overall form, the black space only, and the white space only (pp. 66–67)—for a total of forty-two drawings. She then developed tool paths to feed these drawings to the robots. In one series, she attached a hot-wire cutter to a robot to translate the drawings into forty-eight three-dimensional foam objects at varying scales. In another series, the robot created 412 drawings with "low-fidelity" black felt-tip markers that mechanically traced two different types of paths—either a linear point-to-point movement or an interpolation of a series of points. Besler began to notice idiosyncrasies in each iteration that resulted from the inherent and uncontrollable characteristics of the robots and the effects of speed. Faster movement by the robots produced vibrations that were transmitted to the line, introducing variations within the supposedly identical replications that resulted from this mechanical process.

As it developed, Low Fidelity transformed beyond an analysis of House VI into its own multidimensional project, one that cast a critical eye on technology, questioned the very notion of an exact copy, and explored temporal and mechanical aspects of reproduction. Over the course of the project, Besler created more than 1,200 objects and drawings as well as several videos.[45] As a summary, she made a movie-trailer-like video in which an array of objects, drawings, and footage of the robots at work is presented by a narrator. The video does not reveal the motives behind Besler's creations, but as it moves from the introduction of Eisenman's House VI transformations to

Besler's variations on them, it shows how this project took on a life of its own, and it does so without further reference to the original—despite the fact that the drawings and objects continue to be recognizably related to the drawings of House VI. The many components, when displayed together, convey the breadth of Besler's conversation with history on issues related to representation and the contemporary use of technology.

John Szot Studio

Despite the public nature of buildings and their importance in society, much of the dialogue in architecture remains internal to the discipline. Conversations among practitioners, historians, and theorists seldom engage the broader public. In the speculative video project Architecture and the Unspeakable (2014), John Szot looked outside the field and examined the potential influence of local context and culture on the development of architecture in the belief that some of the most interesting ideas fall beyond the perimeter of standard architectural discourse. Collaborating with Brooklyn Digital Foundry, Szot made a video to explore, as he has described it, "the latent possibilities embedded in the local context," specifically related to three buildings, each in a different city: New York City, Tokyo, and Detroit. For each chapter he constructed a loose narrative around a "pathological"[46] condition mined from the context of the site in order to reveal how the profession might learn from society: "Through the mechanisms of vandalism, idiosyncrasy, and dilapidation, the buildings raise the possibility that architecture might transcend its practical obligations to become our most potent form of cultural expression."[47] As each condition varies, so too does the presentation format.

The first chapter is set in the SoHo neighborhood of New York City, and it highlights vandalism in the form of graffiti and street art (pp. 82–83). In the format of a documentary film, the video begins with shots of an unfinished building left open for several days so that street writers and graffiti artists could participate in its completion. While these collaborators were not formally invited into the site, neither were they discouraged from entering. In fact, contributions were encouraged by elements such as small ledges that provided access to the facade and large concrete walls that acted as blank canvases. The resulting interaction became an integral component of the final inhabited spaces. In the second chapter, Szot looked to idiosyncrasy to produce a residential high-rise with forty-nine unique units in the Shibuya ward of Tokyo (pp. 84–85). The parametric design was computer generated using the context, including the small footprint of the site, the height of a typical building in the neighborhood, and the number and various socioeconomic types of spaces needed. The diagrammatic presentation of this tower simulates a real-estate marketing video, outlining the various amenities and spaces that derive from the unique conditions of the site. The video concludes with views of the inhabited top-floor unit, which looks out through a luminous advertising display that wraps around three sides of the building's top twelve meters, further emphasizing the idiosyncrasies inherent in the local context of Tokyo. The third chapter focuses on Detroit (pp. 86–87). With the city's recent filing for bankruptcy, architectural discourse in Detroit often leans toward revitalization or urban renewal. By contrast, Szot developed a narrative to look at how dilapidation—an inherent characteristic of contemporary Detroit—might inform an approach to architecture in the city. The initial design comprises a series of rooms made of closed concrete masonry that have no windows or doors. Accompanied by a sound track of loud music, spectacular animations depict walls being broken through at random to reveal how destruction would create circulation in the structure.

As someone who embraces digital tools, Szot sees video simulation as an opportunity to rethink design and people's perspectives on the discipline. The narrative structure allows him to test out his theories. As he put it, "Architecture has always been hemmed in by practicality, which is difficult to argue against. But I see filmmaking as a way of exploring ideas that might be a little outside of the acceptable range."[48] His work draws inspiration from a wide range of sources, such as scenographic development in Ridley Scott's early films *Alien* and *Blade Runner* (1979 and 1982, respectively; see fig. 36). A clear influence from architecture is War and Architecture: The Sarajevo Window (1994; see fig. 37) by the visionary architect Lebbeus Woods. Szot shares Woods's belief that architecture could learn a lot from stepping outside the confines of the discipline. As Woods observed some twenty years ago, "The practice of architecture today is protected from confrontation with changing political conditions in the world within a hermetically sealed capsule of professionalism, which ostensibly exists to protect its high standards

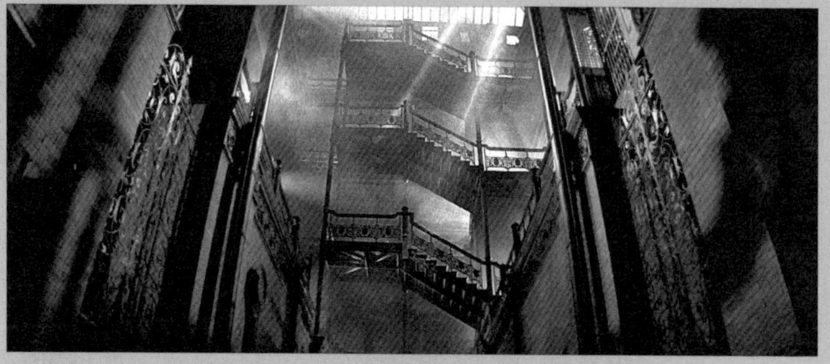

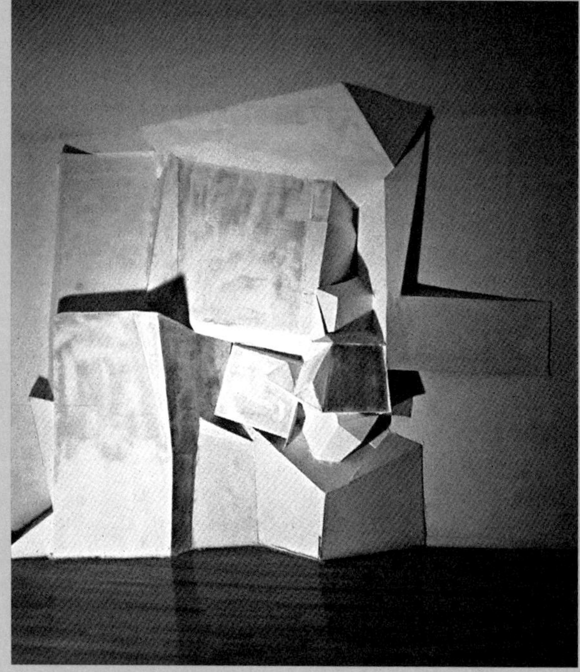

Fig. 36. Ridley Scott, *Blade Runner*, still frame, 1982

Fig. 37. Lebbeus Woods, *Prototypical Wall and Window Repair for Sarajevo, Bosnia, and Herzegovina*, c. 1994

from the corrupting influence of political expediency and merely topical concerns. . . . Professionalism separates architects from people and their need to change the conditions of their existence, which is the essence of all politics."[49]

As time progresses, so do architecture and culture; Szot is interested in finding the confluence between the two. Pioneering modernist architect Adolf Loos, in his 1908 commentary on ornamentation, showed a similar awareness of the need to be attuned to contemporary society: "There is no longer any organic connection between ornament and our culture, ornament is no longer an expression of our culture."[50] Loos's disavowal of ornamentation stemmed from its relationship with technology at the time; he argued that the traditional techniques used to create ornamentation were not modern and therefore not culturally relevant. Like Loos, Szot aims to develop architecture that is conversant with this moment while using tools germane to today's world. The three chapters of Architecture and the Unspeakable propose an alternative approach to architecture and use unique narratives to embrace otherwise overlooked or ephemeral aspects of a culture; the variety in presentation styles parallels the diversity of contemporary media formats.

Together, the five practices featured here represent a dynamic array of conversations, approaches to design, and perspectives on history at work in contemporary architecture today. Concurrent with the emergence of these architects is the expanded role of technology not only as a tool but as a stimulus in shaping the ways architecture is discussed and produced. It is not simply the digital that has influenced the projects discussed here; through the combination of digital tools used in areas from production to communication, these works are largely dependent on their particular moment in history. As philosopher Walter Benjamin said, "The manner in which human sense perception is organized, the medium in which it is accomplished, is determined not only by nature but by historical circumstances as well."[51] The contemporary embrace of technology has created a monumental shift that has affected society as a whole, fostering the proliferation of worldwide networks that cross geographical and political boundaries and at the same time affecting the way individuals interact with one another in their daily lives.

The question of how the impact of current modes of communication might extend to architecture was raised by architectural historian Beatriz Colomina: "In recent years, an unexpected revolution of at least the same significance as the one that brought us photography, film, illustrated magazines, and modern publicity has taken place. The Internet, email, blogs, Google, Twitter, YouTube, Facebook, WikiLeaks, and the like have profoundly changed the way we work, write, analyze, theorize, socialize, interact, play, make love. Can we expect architecture not to be affected?"[52]

The multifarious approaches to architectural discourse and production discussed here represent a talking back to and building on history while developing new conversations informed by and constructed using contemporary technologies and media. This expanded landscape of production and communication is testimony to the pluralism that dominates the field today, with strong references to antecedents and disciplinary contexts. The work of this generation can be read as a form of creative and productive architectural chatter.

John Szot Studio

Architecture and the Unspeakable, 2014

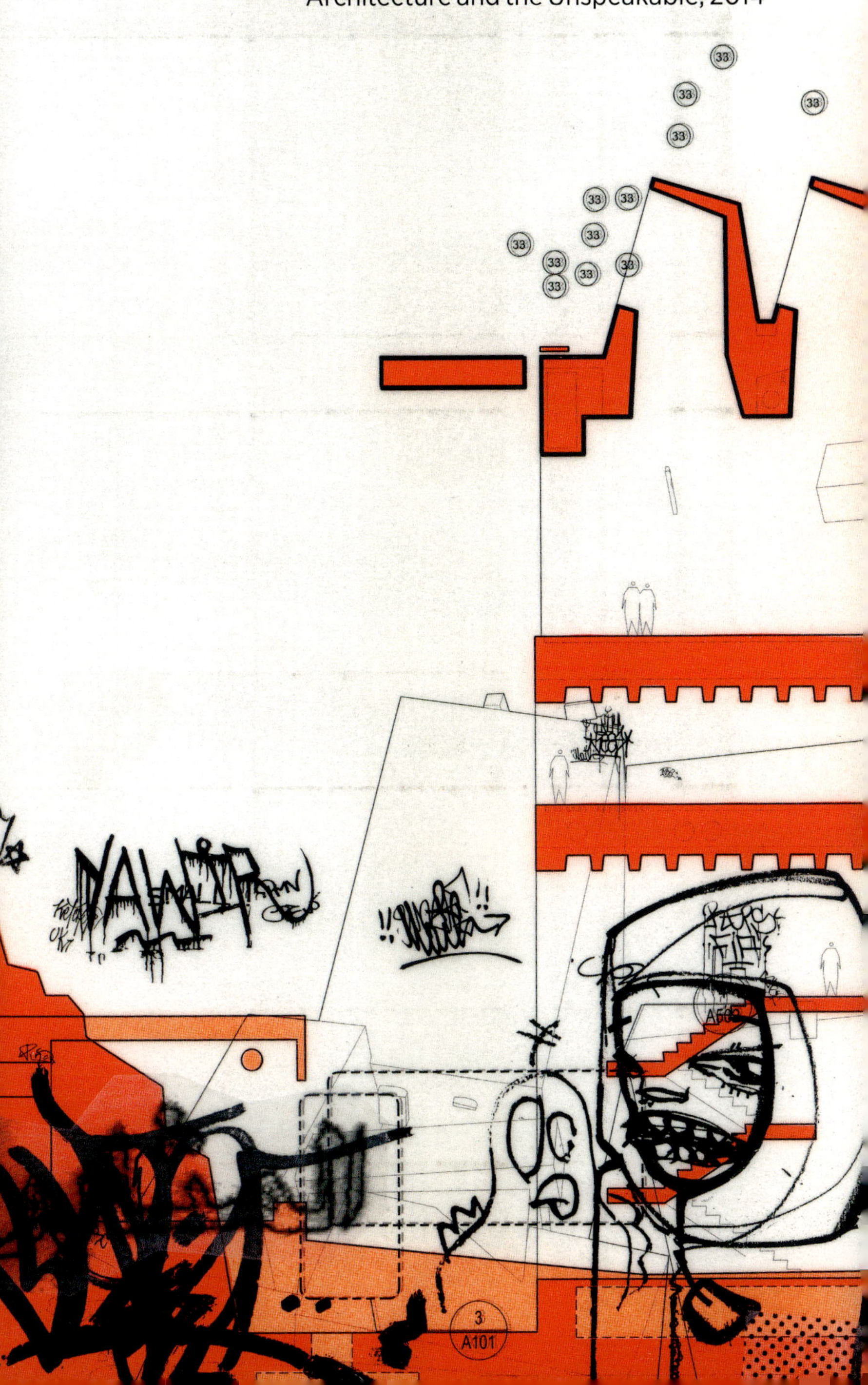

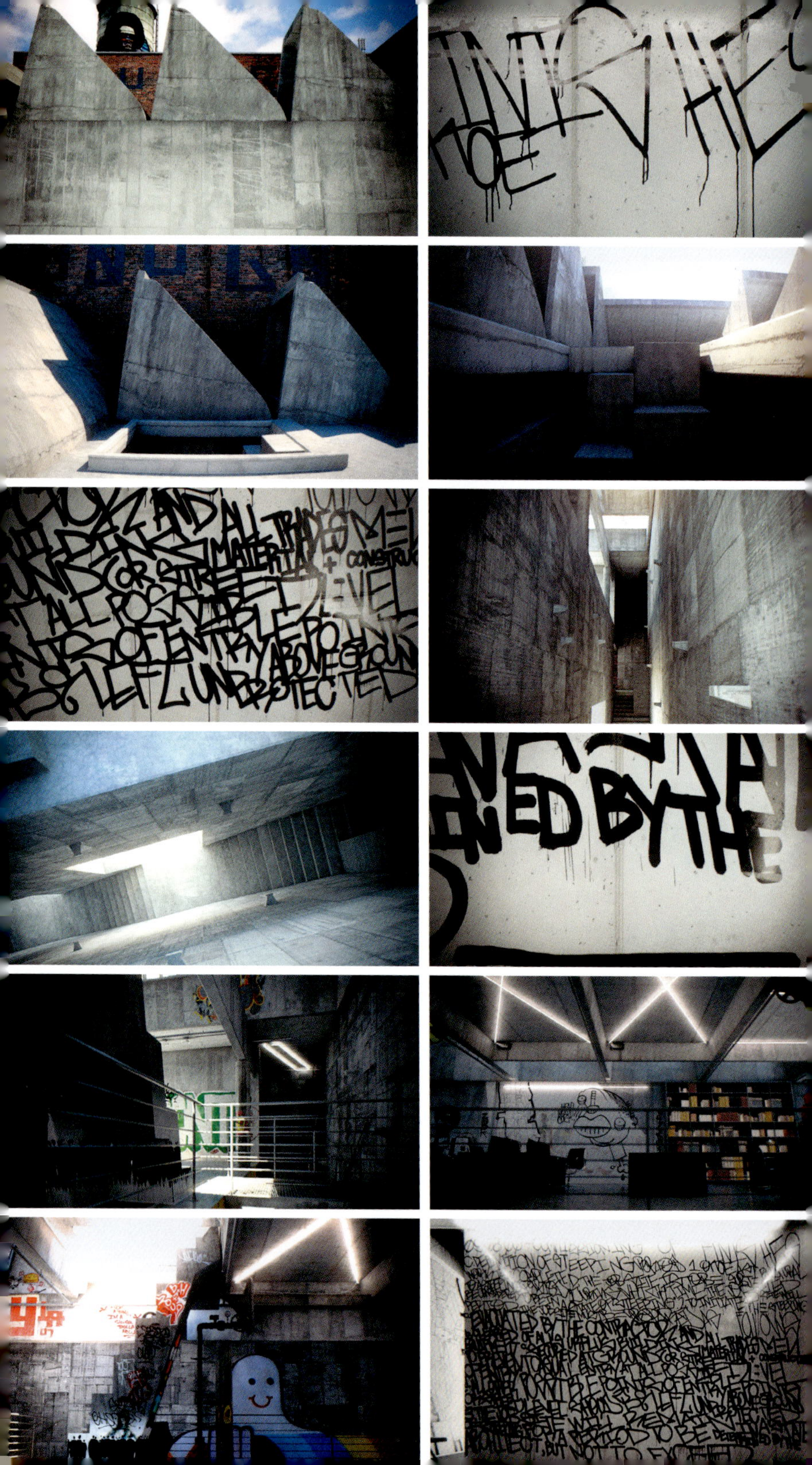

ED BYTHE

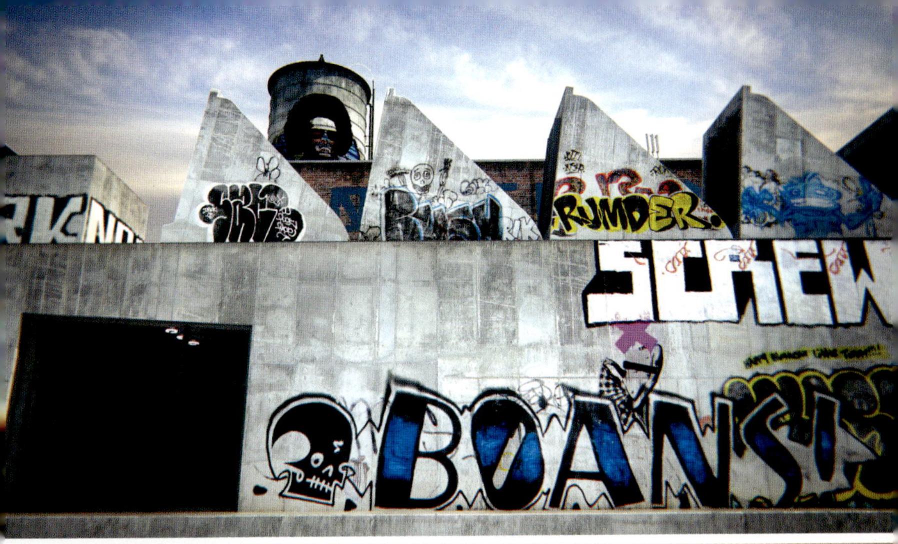

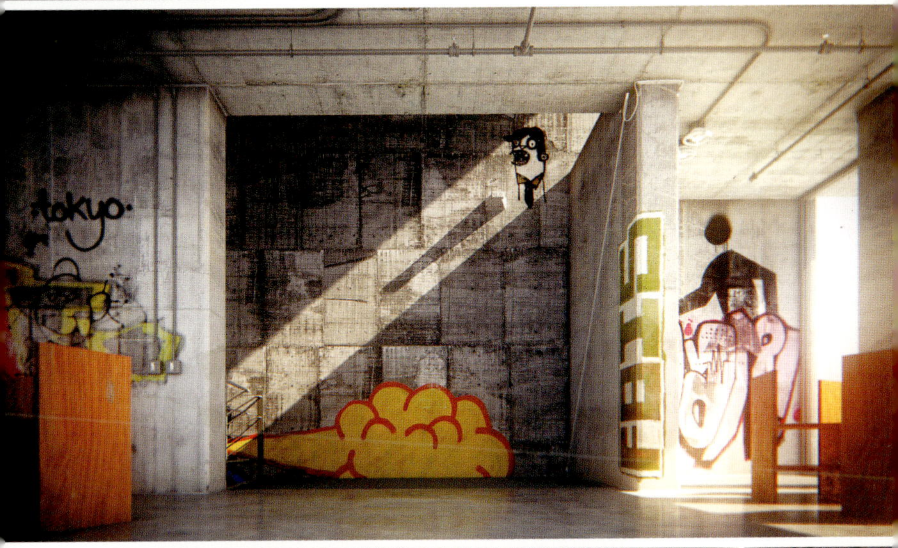

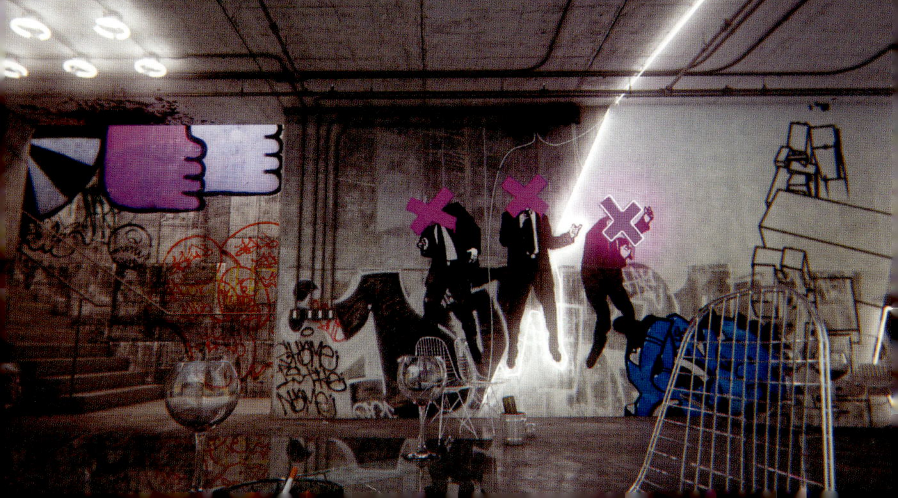

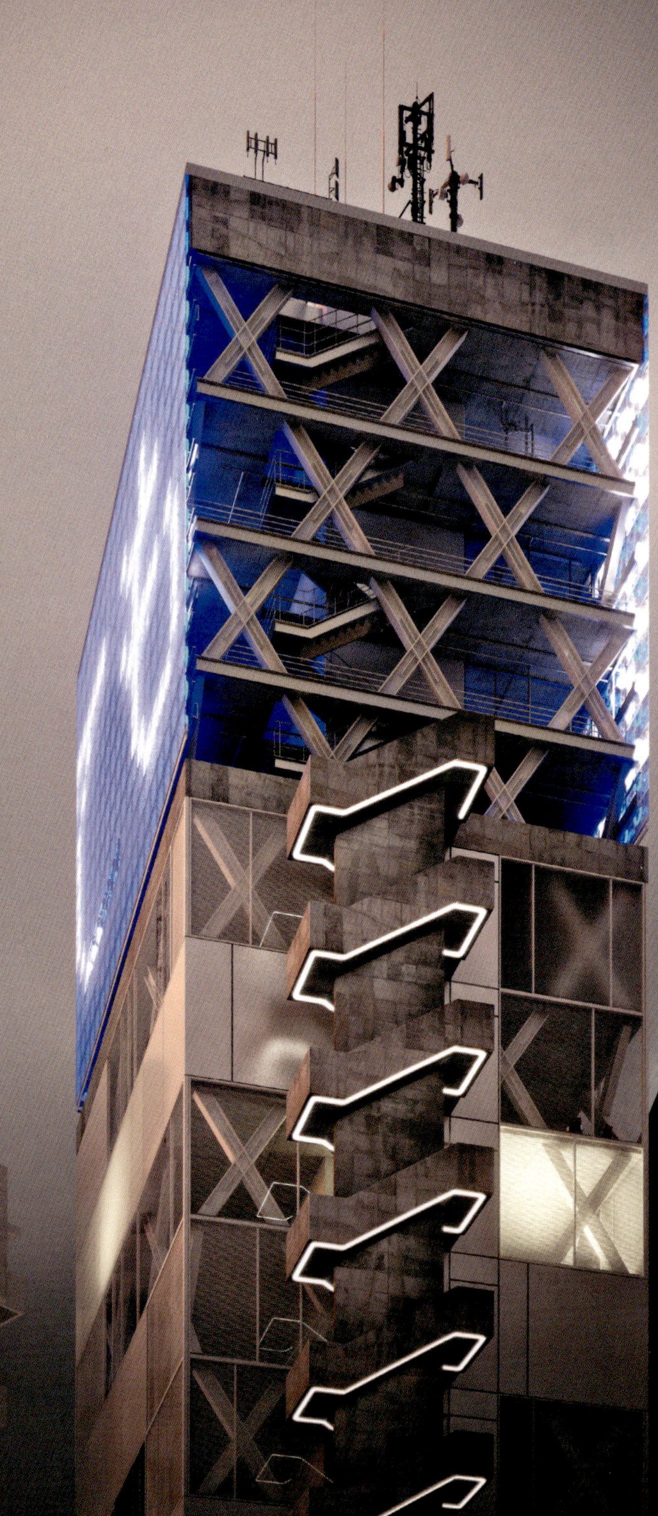

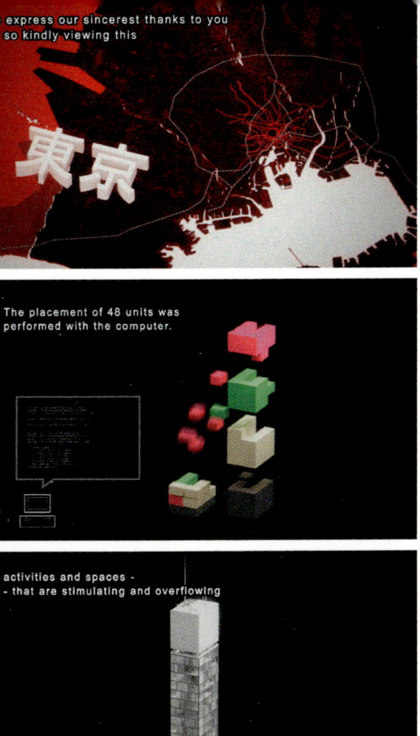

e express our sincerest thanks to you
r so kindly viewing this
東京
The placement of 48 units was
performed with the computer.

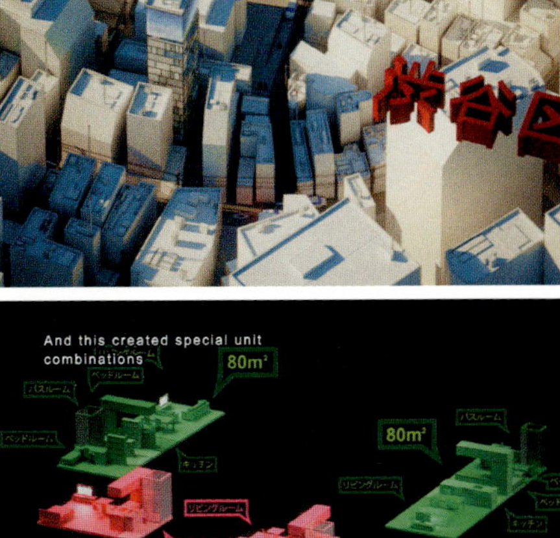

Tokyo's heart.
Here
渋谷区

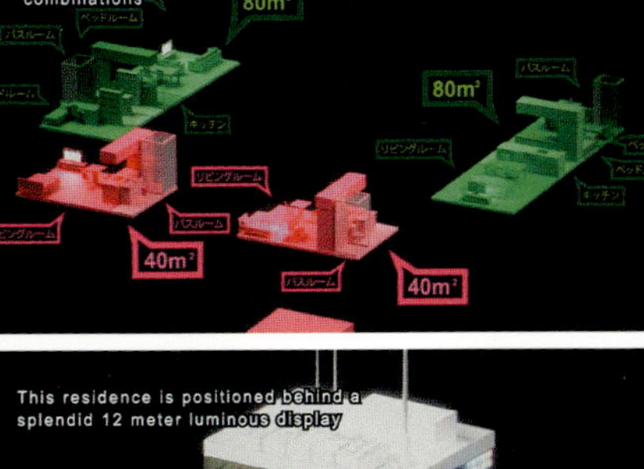

And this created special unit
combinations
80m²
バスルーム
ベッドルーム
キッチン
80m²
バスルーム
リビングルーム
リビングルーム
リビングルーム
バスルーム
40m²
バスルーム
40m²

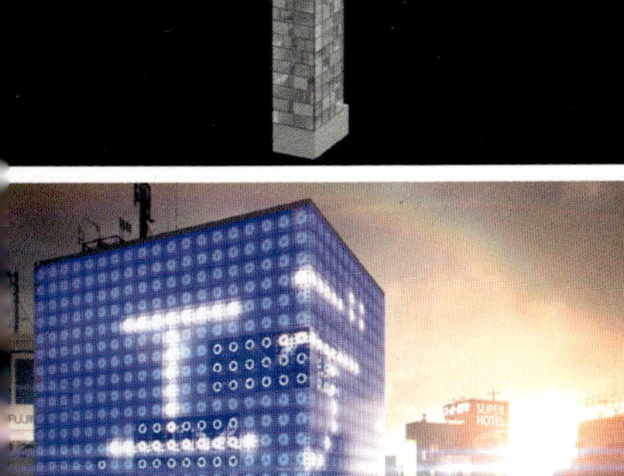

activities and spaces -
- that are stimulating and overflowing

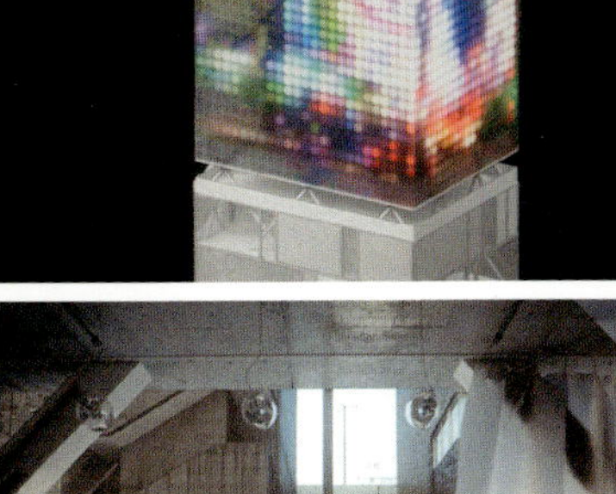

This residence is positioned behind a
splendid 12 meter luminous display

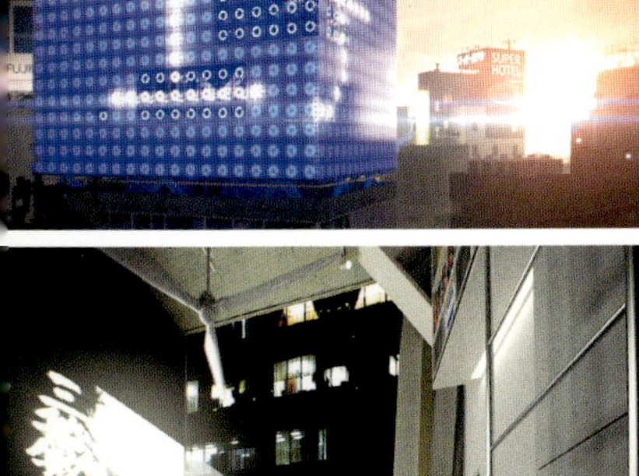

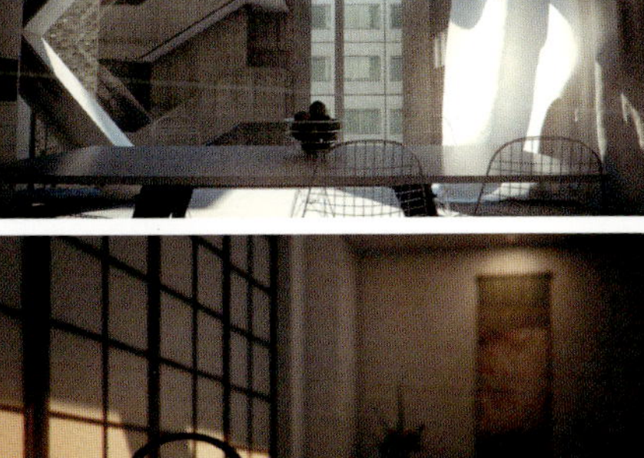

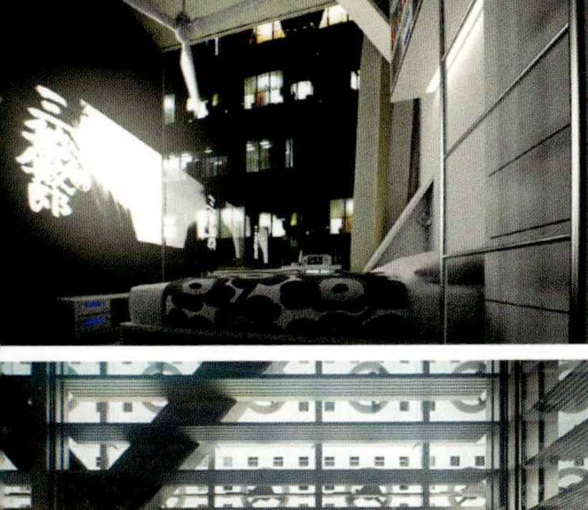

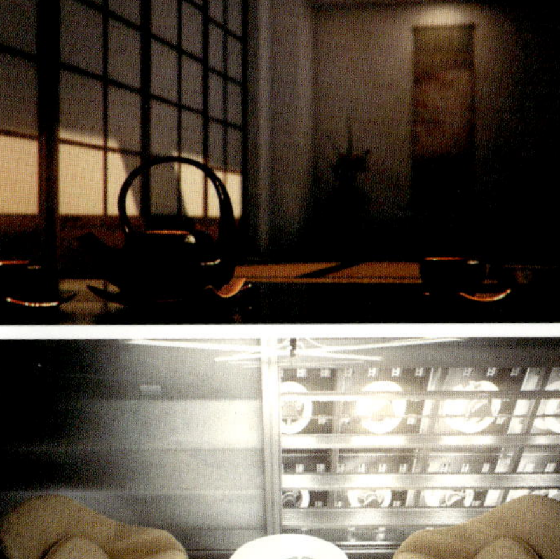

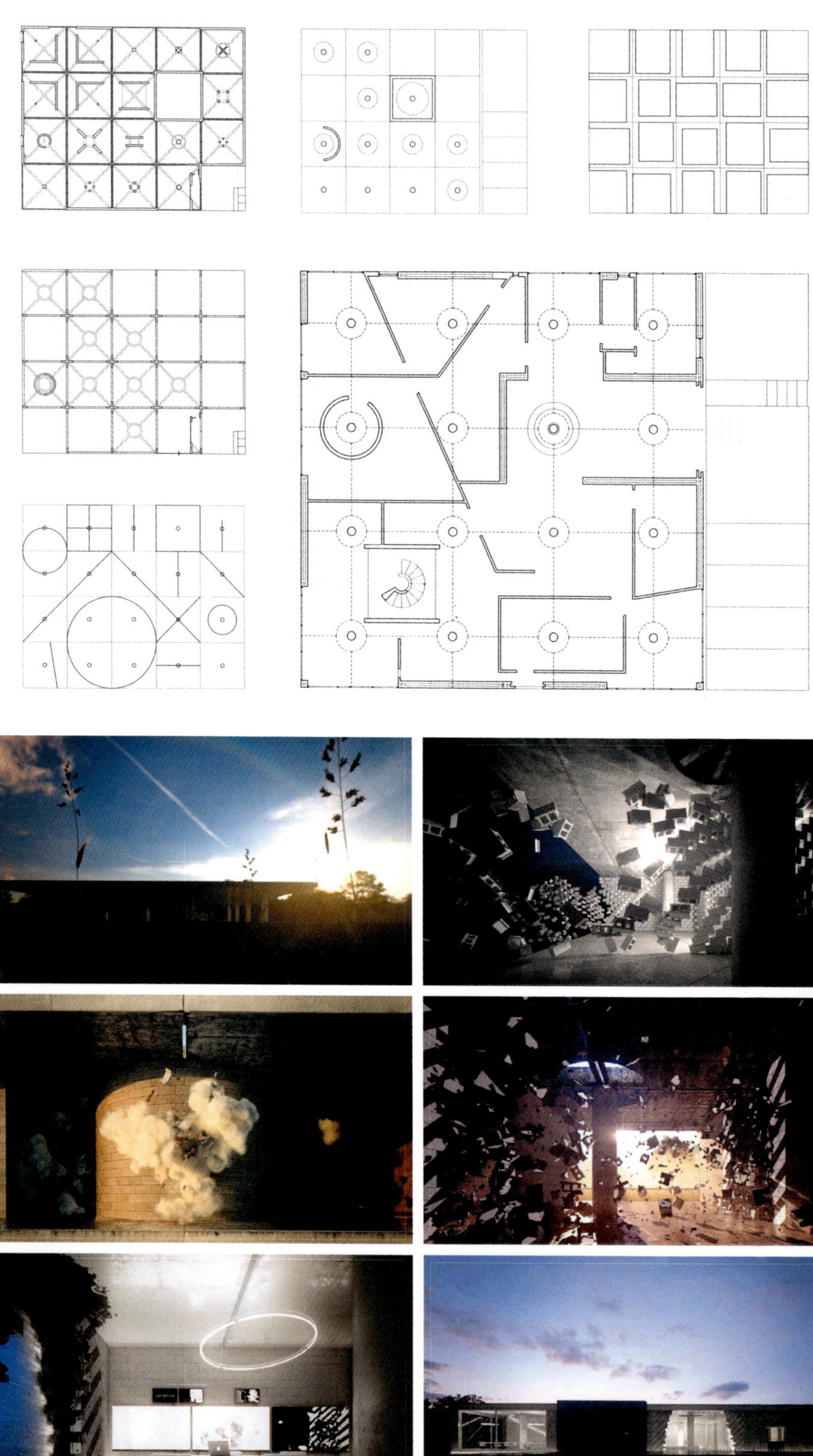

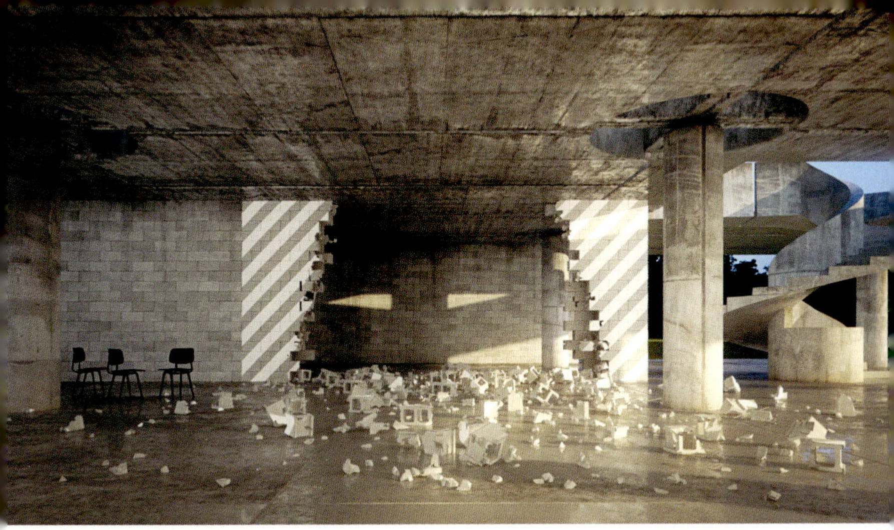

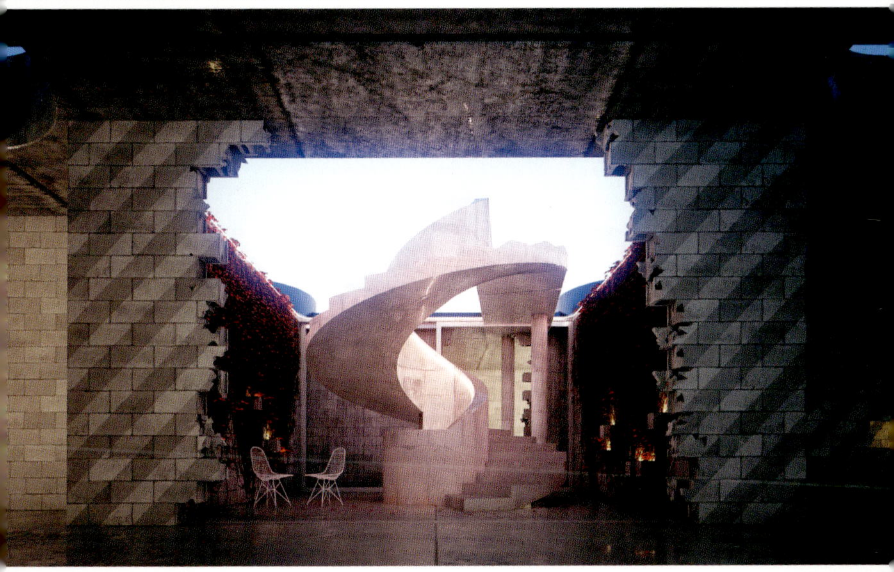

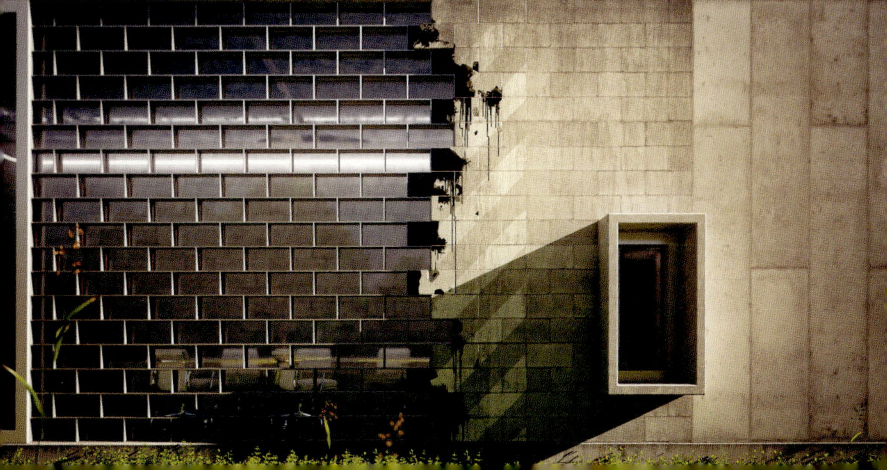

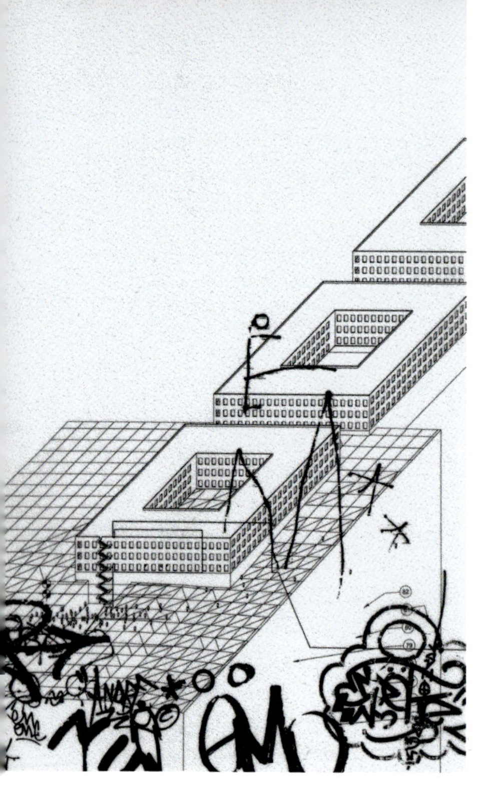

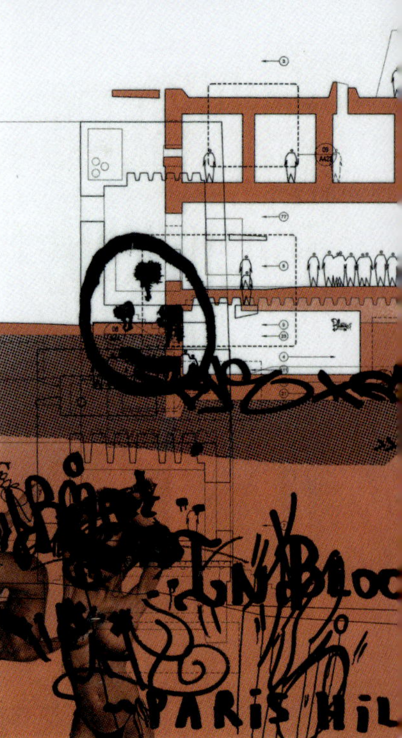

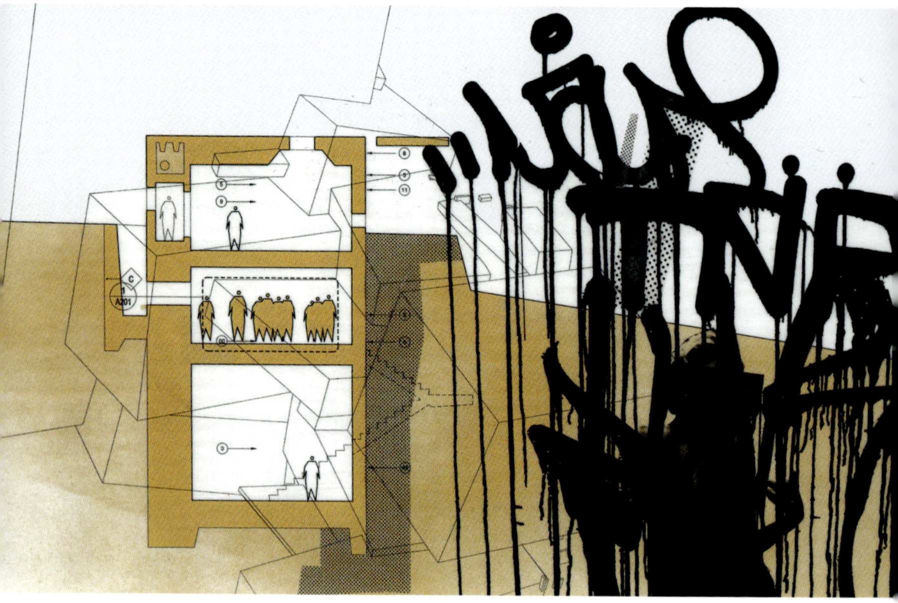

Pages 81, 88: Conceptual drawings

Pages 82–83: Chapter 1, "SoHo," video still frames (left) and digital renderings (right)

Pages 84–85: Chapter 2, "Shibuya," digital rendering (left) and video still frames (right)

Pages 86–87: Chapter 3, "Detroit," floor plans (top left), video still frames (bottom left), and digital renderings (right)

Notes

1. This pluralism is in contrast to the milieu in the early part of the twentieth century, when distinct movements such as the International Style (exemplified by the Museum of Modern Art's 1932 exhibition by Henry-Russell Hitchcock and Philip Johnson) were dominant in the field.

2. In recent years, the emergence of ominous references to terrorist chatter gathered from the surveillance of communication outlets has lent a new importance to the kind of content related to this term.

3. Richard Kearney, *On Stories* (Routledge, 2002), p. 4.

4. James S. Ackerman, "Introduction: The Conventions and Rhetoric of Architectural Drawing," in *Conventions of Architectural Drawing: Representation and Misrepresentation*, ed. James S. Ackerman and Wolfgang Jung (Harvard University Graduate School of Design, 2000), p. 36.

5. Sylvia Lavin, "Filling In the Blank," *A+U: Architecture and Urbanism* 8, 251 (Aug. 1991), p. 82.

6. The modernist notion that form follows function prescribed that the form of the architecture should indicate its functions, rather than being guided by ornamentation or style.

7. Robert Venturi, Denise Scott Brown, and Steven Izenour, *Learning from Las Vegas* (MIT Press, 1977), pp. 135–36.

8. Unlike architects of the Prairie School, such as Frank Lloyd Wright, who were inspired to incorporate architecture into its natural surroundings, Le Corbusier was influenced by industrial machinery and saw architecture as a "machine for living" that should contrast with nature—a relationship described as a machine in the garden. This notion was set forth by Le Corbusier in his seminal 1923 publication *Vers une architecture* and is manifest in his design for Villa Savoye (1931). See Le Corbusier, *Towards a New Architecture*, trans. Frederick Etchells (1927; repr., Dover, 1986).

9. In the case of Tigerman's Bloch Residence, the imposition of symmetry on the design of the facade privileged style over form, rather than letting the function dictate the form of the house. In this way, Tigerman's design was a bold statement against modernism.

10. Dora Epstein Jones and Bryony Roberts, eds., "New Ancients," *Log* 31 (Spring/Summer 2014), pp. 11–12.

11. Hal Foster, "(Post) Modern Polemics," *Perspecta* 21 (Jan. 1984), p. 149.

12. Louis H. Sullivan, *Kindergarten Chats and Other Writings* (1918; repr., Dover, 1979).

13. Vinciarelli moved to Marfa, Texas, to work alongside the Minimalist artist Donald Judd. The town of Marfa became an enclave of Minimalist art and architecture due to Judd's move there in the 1970s.

14. In 1980 Stuart Cohen, Rhona Hoffman, and Stanley Tigerman organized an exhibition at the Museum of Contemporary Art in Chicago titled *Late Entries to the Chicago Tribune Tower Competition*, inviting contemporary architects to submit designs for the famous 1922 competition. Stanley Tigerman, *Late Entries to the Chicago Tribune Tower Competition* (Rizzoli, 1980).

15. Stan Allen, "From Object to Field: Field Conditions in Architecture and Urbanism," in *Space Reader: Heterogeneous Space in Architecture*, ed. Michael Hensel, Christopher Hight, and Achim Menges (Wiley, 2009), p. 140.

16. In 1992, as part of the curriculum at Columbia University's Graduate School of Architecture, Preservation, and Planning, Greg Lynn and Hani Rashid developed a "paperless studio," one of the first attempts in this context to enforce the use of computers in architectural design. Antoine Picon, *Digital Culture in Architecture: An Introduction for the Design Professions* (Birkhäuser, 2010), p. 8.

17. Mario Carpo, "Ten Years of Folding," in *Folding in Architecture*, ed. Greg Lynn (Academy Press, 2004), p. 16.

18. Greg Lynn, "The End of 'In the Future,'" in *Archaeology of the Digital*, ed. Greg Lynn, exh. cat. (Canadian Centre for Architecture/Sternberg Press, 2013; repr., Ram, 2014), p. 11.

19. Jonathan Crary, *24/7: Late Capitalism and the Ends of Sleep* (Verso, 2013), p. 35.

20. Picon, *Digital Culture in Architecture*, p. 9.

21. Crary, *24/7*, p. 39.

22. The work of Archigram aimed to insert ideas into and draw inspiration from contemporary mass culture. This approach is made plain in founder Peter Cook's famous comment, "The pre-packaged frozen lunch is more important than Palladio. For one thing it is more basic. It is an expression of human requirement and the symbol of an efficient interpretation of that requirement that optimizes the available technology and economy." Their name was developed from the notion of architecture telegrams—small pamphlets they published from 1961 to 1974 as a way to disseminate their ideas. Lara Schrijver, *Radical Games: Popping the Bubble of 1960s Architecture* (NAi, 2009), pp. 95–96. Their use of cartoonlike collage imagery parallels their attempt to draw from and infiltrate contemporary society. This approach can be read as directly influencing Jimenez Lai in the way he has developed his own approachable cartoonish style to deliver rich concepts and build on history.

23. Jimenez Lai, *Citizens of No Place: An Architectural Graphic Novel* (Princeton Architectural Press, 2012), p. 12.

24. Le Corbusier's "Five Points of Modern Architecture" is described in Deborah Gans, *The Le Corbusier Guide*, 3rd ed. (Princeton Architectural Press, 2006), p. 261.

25. Bernard Tschumi Architects, *The Manhattan Transcripts*, www.tschumi.com/projects/18/.

26. Bernard Tschumi, *The Manhattan Transcripts: Theoretical Projects* (St. Martin's Press, 1995), quoted in Mark Garcia, *The Diagrams of Architecture* (Wiley, 2010), p. 198.

27. David Joselit, *After Art*, Point: Essays on Architecture (Princeton University Press, 2013), p. 94.

28. Formlessfinder, "Besides Form," in *Formless*, ed. Garrett Ricciardi and Julian Rose, Storefront for Art and Architecture Manifesto Series 1 (Lars Müller, 2013), pp. 102–03.

29. Ibid., p. 105.

30. Yves-Alain Bois and Rosalind E. Krauss, *Formless: A User's Guide*, exh. cat. (Centre Georges Pompidou / Zone, 1997), p. 18.

31. Formlessfinder, www.formlessfinder.com/about.

32. Projects by Ricciardi and Rose are not generated automatically, but the formlessfinder application aids them in their process, and their reliance on and use of it vary by project.

33. In a sense, this sand was diverted from the supply chain for the pavilion, something that Formlessfinder is interested in exploring; the overlap between materials and resources in the local context of their projects often helps to drive the initial design concept, as was the case with Tent Pile.

34. Bois and Krauss, *Formless*, p. 187.

35. Fake Industries, *Fake Industries Architectural Agonism*, www.fakeindustries.org.

36. Jeanne Silverthorne, quoted in Howard Singerman, *Art History: After Sherrie Levine* (University of California Press, 2012), p. 97.

37. Rooms: No Vacancy project description, www.moma.org/interactives/exhibitions/yap/2014ny_fiaa.html.

38. Radical Italian architects Superstudio and Archizoom were known for their distinctive collage technique in which they referenced modernism through the use of the grid, as seen in Superstudio's Histograms of Architecture (1969–2000) and Archizoom's No-Stop City (1969). Jane Alison et al., eds., *Future City: Experiment and Utopia in Architecture* (Thames and Hudson, 2007), p. 143. Several of the images by Fake Industries use the same approach: a collage of pictures and the appearance of a uniform grid.

39. See Rem Koolhaas, Office for Metropolitan Architecture, et al., "The Chicago School," in *Content*, ed. Rem Koolhaas and Brendan McGetrick (Taschen, 2004), pp. 184–88. Koolhaas used exposed drywall in projects prior to IIT's McCormick Tribune Campus Center, including Prada Epicenter (2001) in New York City.

40. Rem Koolhaas, "Junkspace," *October* 100 (Spring 2002), p. 175.

41. Ibid., p. 185.

42. Robin Evans, "Translations from Drawing to Building," *AAfiles: Annals of the Architectural Association School of Architecture* 12 (Summer 1986), p. 3.

43. Luca Galofaro and Peter Eisenman, *Digital Eisenman: An Office of the Electronic Era*, trans. Lucinda Byatt (Birkhäuser, 1999), p. 85.

44. Jeffrey Kipnis, *Perfect Acts of Architecture*, exh. cat. (Museum of Modern Art, 2001), p. 34.

45. Videos and other images from the project are available on Besler's Web site: www.erinbesler.com/index.php/low-fidelity/.

46. The term *pathological* is one used by Szot to describe this process; for him, it is a sickness that takes over the project.

47. John Szot Studio, *Architecture and the Unspeakable*, johnszot.com/archandtheunspeakable/.

48. John Szot, quoted in Avinash Rajagopal, "Moving Image," *Metropolis* 33, 3 (Oct. 2013), p. 81.

49. Lebbeus Woods, *Anarchitecture: Architecture Is a Political Act* (Academy Editions, 1992), p. 9.

50. Adolf Loos, *Ornament and Crime: Selected Essays*, trans. Michael Mitchell (Ariadne Press, 1998), p. 171.

51. Walter Benjamin, "The Work of Art in the Age of Mechanical Reproduction," quoted in Beatriz Colomina, *Privacy and Publicity* (MIT Press, 1994), p. 17.

52. Beatriz Colomina, "Manifesto Architecture," in *After the Manifesto*, ed. Craig Buckley (Graduate School of Architecture, Preservation, and Planning at Columbia University, 2014), p. 58.

Biographies

Bureau Spectacular's Jimenez Lai is a faculty member in the Department of Architecture and Urban Design at the University of California, Los Angeles. He holds a master's degree in architecture from the University of Toronto. He has lived and worked in a desert shelter at Taliesin West and in a shipping container at Atelier Van Lieshout on the piers of Rotterdam. Before founding Bureau Spectacular, Lai worked for various international firms, including the Office for Metropolitan Architecture. Lai has built numerous installations, such as *White Elephant* (Museum of Modern Art, New York, 2011), and has been widely exhibited and published around the world. His first manifesto, *Citizens of No Place*, was published by Princeton Architectural Press with a grant from the Graham Foundation. The second draft of this book has been archived at the New Museum, New York, as part of the show *The Generational: Younger Than Jesus*. In 2012 Lai won the Architectural League Prize for Young Architects. He was the recipient of the Début Award at the Lisbon Architecture Triennale in 2013. Lai was the curator and designer of the 2014 Taiwan Pavilion at the 14th International Architecture Exhibition at the Venice Biennale.

Formlessfinder was created by Garrett Ricciardi and Julian Rose and exists as the nexus of their ongoing collaboration. The studio operates as a "finder" in the sense of a search engine, fluidly analyzing a wide range of information and producing diverse outputs (buildings, pictures, videos, models, texts, products, data, software). In this new way of working, unexpected collaborations emerge and traditional understandings of and distinctions between media disappear: video becomes a form of drawing, software a kind of theoretical discourse, and conversation the output of a design process. Formlessfinder won the 2012 AIA NY New Practices New York competition, received a 2012 National Endowment for the Arts grant, and was selected as a finalist for the MoMA PS1 Young Architects Program in 2011. Their design work, ranging from residential additions to public pavilions, has been exhibited at institutions such as the Museum of Modern Art in New York, the MAXXI in Rome, the Storefront for Art and Architecture in New York, and Design Miami and has been featured in numerous publications, including *Architectural Record*, *Domus*, *Surface Magazine*, *Metropolis*, *W Magazine*, and *Vogue*, among others. In 2013 Formlessfinder published their first book, *Formless*, with Lars Müller Publishers and the Storefront for Art and Architecture.

Fake Industries Architectural Agonism is an entity of variable boundaries and questionable taste that provides architectural tools to mediate between citizens and institutions, the public sphere and disciplinary knowledge. Created by Cristina Goberna and Urtzi Grau and headquartered in New York, Sydney, and Barcelona, Fake Industries bridges the gap between the professional world and architectural academia to reclaim the architect's role as a public intellectual—that is, someone who earnestly risks his or her credibility to question hegemonic beliefs. Currently completing the velodrome in Medellín, Colombia; the Superphosphates! Master Plan in Cáceres, Spain; and the OE House in Barcelona, for the past eight years the firm has consistently used its winning entries for the Europan competition (eighth through eleventh editions) to explore the domestic dreams of the south of Europe. In 2014 Fake Industries won the AIA NY New Practices New York competition and was shortlisted for the MoMA PS1 Young Architects Program, Art Basel Miami Beach, and the Guggenheim Helsinki Design Competition.

Erin Besler was born in Chicago, Illinois. She is a faculty member in the Department of Architecture and Urban Design at the University of California, Los Angeles, where she was the 2013–14 Teaching Fellow. She holds a bachelor of arts degree from Yale University and a master's degree in architecture with distinction from the Southern California Institute of Architecture. She has worked at Tigerman McCurry Architects and VOA Associates in Chicago, and First Office and Zago Architecture in Los Angeles. Her work has been presented internationally in association with the Digital Architecture Design Association (DADA) at Beijing Design Week 2013 and as part of Advances in Architectural Geometry in 2012 at the Centre Pompidou in Paris. Recently, her work has been exhibited in Los Angeles at Design Matters Gallery, the MAK Center for Art and Architecture's Mackey Garage-Top Gallery, the Neutra VDL House, the Architecture and Design Museum, and Jai & Jai Gallery. She was selected as a finalist for the 2015 MoMA PS1 Young Architects Program. Her work has been published in *San Rocco*, *Future Anterior*, and *Project*.

John Szot is an award-winning architect based in Brooklyn, New York. His design practice—John Szot Studio—is focused on exploring the relationship between technology and meaning in the built environment. In 1999 he cofounded the Brooklyn Digital Foundry, a multimedia design studio that has gone on to work with a wide range of prestigious clients in industries as diverse as fashion, the arts, architecture, and finance. Szot's writings, drawings, and interviews have appeared in numerous publications, including *Metropolis*, *Archinect*, *Designboom*, *Faesthetic*, *CLOG*, *Pidgin*, *Soiled*, *Design Taxi*, and *MAS Context*, and his architectural work has been exhibited internationally. In addition to providing creative and conceptual direction at his studio and for Brooklyn Digital Foundry, he teaches advanced architectural design and filmmaking at Columbia University, the University of Texas at Austin, and the Pratt Institute. He recently completed the short video *Architecture and the Unspeakable*, featuring a triptych of architectural proposals exploring the cultural potential of building pathology, and the corresponding book—a collection of related essays and drawings—is planned for 2015.

Selected Bibliography

Ackerman, James S. "Introduction: The Conventions and Rhetoric of Architectural Drawing." In *Conventions of Architectural Drawing: Representation and Misrepresentation*, ed. James S. Ackerman and Wolfgang Jung, pp. 8–36. Harvard University Graduate School of Design, 2000.

Alison, Jane, Marie-Ange Brayer, Frédéric Migayrou, and Neil Spiller, eds. *Future City: Experiment and Utopia in Architecture*. Thames and Hudson, 2007.

Allen, Stan. "From Object to Field: Field Conditions in Architecture and Urbanism." In *Space Reader: Heterogeneous Space in Architecture*, ed. Michael Hensel, Christopher Hight, and Achim Menges, pp. 118–44. Wiley, 2009.

Antonelli, Paola. *Design and the Elastic Mind*. Exh. cat. Museum of Modern Art, 2008.

——. *Talk to Me: Design and the Communication between People and Objects*. Exh. cat. Museum of Modern Art, 2011.

Bal, Mieke. *The Point of Theory*. Continuum, 1994.

Benjamin, Walter. "The Work of Art in the Age of Mechanical Reproduction." In *Illuminations*, pp. 217–51. Translated by Harry Zohn. Schocken, 2007.

Bois, Yves-Alain, and Rosalind E. Krauss. *Formless: A User's Guide*. Exh. cat. Centre Georges Pompidou / Zone, 1997.

Brilliant, Richard, and Dale Kinney. *Reuse Value*. Ashgate, 2011.

Carpo, Mario. "Ten Years of Folding." In *Folding in Architecture*, ed. Greg Lynn, pp. 14–19. Academy Press, 2004.

Choi, Esther, and Marrikka Trotter. *Architecture at the Edge of Everything Else*. MIT Press, 2010.

Coates, Nigel. *Narrative Architecture*. Wiley, 2012.

Colomina, Beatriz. "Manifesto Architecture." In *After the Manifesto*, ed. Craig Buckley, pp. 38–59. Graduate School of Architecture, Preservation, and Planning at Columbia University, 2014.

——. *Privacy and Publicity*. MIT Press, 1994.

Colquhoun, Alan. *Essays in Architectural Criticism: Modern Architecture and Historical Change*. MIT Press, 1981.

Crary, Jonathan. *24/7: Late Capitalism and the Ends of Sleep*. Verso, 2013.

Eisenman, Peter. *Diagram Diaries*. Universe, 1999.

——. *Eisenman Inside Out*. Yale University Press, 2004.

Engeli, Maia. *Digital Stories: The Poetics of Communication*. Birkhäuser, 2000.

Epstein Jones, Dora, and Bryony Roberts, eds. "New Ancients." *Log* 31 (Spring/Summer 2014).

Evans, Robin. "Translations from Drawing to Building." *AAfiles: Annals of the Architectural Association School of Architecture* 12 (Summer 1986), pp. 3–18.

Formlessfinder. "Besides Form." In *Formless*, ed. Garrett Ricciardi and Julian Rose, pp. 97–115. Storefront for Art and Architecture Manifesto Series 1. Lars Müller, 2013.

Foster, Hal. "(Post) Modern Polemics." *Perspecta* 21 (Jan. 1984), pp. 144–53.

Frampton, Kenneth. *Modern Architecture: A Critical History*. Thames and Hudson, 1980.

Galofaro, Luca, and Peter Eisenman. *Digital Eisenman: An Office of the Electronic Era*. Translated by Lucinda Byatt. Birkhäuser, 1999.

Gans, Deborah. *The Le Corbusier Guide*. 3rd ed. Princeton Architectural Press, 2006.

Garcia, Mark. *The Diagrams of Architecture*. Wiley, 2010.

Gil, Iker, ed. *Mas Context: Communication* 14 (Summer 2012).

——, ed. *Mas Context: Information* 7 (Fall 2010).

Hvattum, Mari, and Christian Hermansen. *Tracing Modernity: Manifestations of the Modern in Architecture and the City*. Routledge, 2004.

Jencks, Charles. *Modern Movements in Architecture*. Anchor Press, 1973.

——. *The Story of Post-Modernism: Five Decades of the Ironic, Iconic, and Critical in Architecture*. Wiley, 2011.

Joselit, David. *After Art*. Point: Essays on Architecture. Princeton University Press, 2013.

Kearney, Richard. *On Stories*. Routledge, 2002.

Kipnis, Jeffrey. *Perfect Acts of Architecture*. Exh. cat. Museum of Modern Art, 2001.

——. *A Question of Qualities*. MIT Press, 2013.

Koolhaas, Rem. *Delirious New York*. 010 Publishers, 1994.

——. "Junkspace." *October* 100 (Spring 2002), pp. 175–90.

Koolhaas, Rem, Office for Metropolitan Architecture, et al. "The Chicago School." In *Content*, ed. Rem Koolhaas and Brendan McGetrick, pp. 184–88. Taschen, 2004.

Lai, Jimenez. *Citizens of No Place: An Architectural Graphic Novel*. Princeton Architectural Press, 2012.

Lang, Peter, and William Menking. *Superstudio: Life without Objects*. Skira Editore, 2003.

Latour, Bruno. *We Have Never Been Modern*. Harvard University Press, 1993.

Lavin, Sylvia. "Filling In the Blank." *A+U: Architecture and Urbanism* 8, 251 (Aug. 1991), pp. 80–116.

Le Corbusier. *Towards a New Architecture*. Translated and with an introduction by Frederick Etchells. John Rodker, 1927. Reprint, Dover, 1986.

Loos, Adolf. *Ornament and Crime: Selected Essays*. Translated by Michael Mitchell. Ariadne Press, 1998.

Lynn, Greg. "The End of 'In the Future.'" In *Archaeology of the Digital*, ed. Greg Lynn, pp. 11–19. Exh. cat. Canadian Centre for Architecture/Sternberg Press, 2013. Reprint, Ram, 2014.

Lynn, Greg, and Hani Rashid. *Architectural Laboratories*. NAi, 2002.

Miljački, Ana, Amanda R. Lawrence, and Ashley Schafer, eds. "True Stories." *Praxis: Journal of Writing and Building* 14 (2013).

Mitchell, William. *City of Bits*. MIT Press, 1995.

Pallasmaa, Juhani. *The Embodied Image*. Wiley, 2011.

Picon, Antoine. *Digital Culture in Architecture: An Introduction for the Design Professions*. Birkhäuser, 2010.

Rajagopal, Avinash. "Moving Image." *Metropolis* 33, 3 (Oct. 2013), pp. 80–81.

Sadler, Simon. *Archigram: Architecture without Architecture*. MIT Press, 2005.

Schrijver, Lara. *Radical Games: Popping the Bubble of 1960s Architecture*. NAi, 2009.

Shields, Jennifer. *Collage and Architecture*. Routledge, 2014.

Singerman, Howard. *Art History: After Sherrie Levine*. University of California Press, 2012.

Sullivan, Louis H. *Kindergarten Chats and Other Writings*. 1918. Reprint, Dover, 1979.

Tigerman, Stanley. *Late Entries to the Chicago Tribune Tower Competition*. Rizzoli, 1980.

Tschumi, Bernard. *Architecture and Disjunction*. MIT Press, 1994.

——. *The Manhattan Transcripts: Theoretical Projects*. St. Martin's Press, 1995.

Venturi, Robert, and Denise Scott Brown. *Architecture as Signs and Systems*. Harvard University Press, 2004.

Venturi, Robert, Denise Scott Brown, and Steven Izenour. *Learning from Las Vegas*. MIT Press, 1977.

Vidler, Anthony. *Histories of the Immediate Present*. MIT Press, 2008.

Woods, Lebbeus. *Anarchitecture: Architecture Is a Political Act*. Academy Editions, 1992.

Photography Credits

Unless otherwise noted, all photographs of artworks appear by permission of the lenders mentioned in the captions. Every effort has been made to contact and acknowledge copyright holders for all reproductions; additional rights holders are encouraged to contact the Art Institute of Chicago. The following credits apply to all images in this catalogue for which separate acknowledgment is due.

Unless otherwise noted, all photographs of works owned by the Art Institute of Chicago were made by the Department of Imaging, Louis Meluso, Director of Imaging Technology, Christopher Gallagher, Director of Photography, and are copyrighted by the Art Institute of Chicago.

Fig. 1: Art Institute of Chicago; gift of Robert Venturi through Mr. and Mrs. Jay A. Pritzker, 1996.39. **Fig. 2**: Art Institute of Chicago; gift of Stanley Tigerman, 2012.629. **Figs. 3, 4**: © Charles Jencks. **Fig. 5**: Art Institute of Chicago; gift of Stuart Cohen, 2012.607. **Fig. 6**: Art Institute of Chicago; gift of Rhona Hoffman, 2012.479. **Fig. 7**: © Skidmore, Owings & Merrill LLP. **Fig. 8**: Art Institute of Chicago; gift of Walter A. Netsch, Jr., 1989.455.5. **Fig. 9**: Art Institute of Chicago; funds provided by the Architecture & Design Society, 2011.260. **Fig. 10**: Art Institute of Chicago; funds provided by the Architecture & Design Society, 2011.256. **Fig. 11**: Art Institute of Chicago; funds provided by the Architecture & Design Society, 2013.78.2. **Fig. 12**: Art Institute of Chicago; funds provided by the Architecture & Design Society, 2013.78.24. **P. 38** (bottom): Photography by Tim Parsons. **P. 39**: Photography by James Harris. **Fig. 13**: Art Institute of Chicago; Department of Architecture and Design Purchase Fund, 2006.311. **Fig. 14**: © 2015 Artists Rights Society (ARS), New York / DACS, London, for the Ron Herron Archive. **Fig. 16**: Art Institute of Chicago; gift of Stanley Tigerman, 1983.692. **Fig. 17**: Courtesy Fondazione Aldo Rossi. **Fig. 23**: © SANAA. **Fig. 24**: Photography by Liao Yusheng. **Fig. 26**: Photography by Rob 't Hart. **Fig. 27**: Museum of Modern Art, New York; purchase and partial gift of the architect in honor of Lily Auchincloss. Digital image © The Museum of Modern Art / Licensed by SCALA / Art Resource, NY. **P. 49**: Courtesy of Córdova & Canillas. **P. 50**: Courtesy of Luis Urculo. **Pp. 52–53**: Collages courtesy of Córdova & Canillas. **Pp. 54–55**: Courtesy of Luis Urculo. **P. 56**: Courtesy of Córdova & Canillas. **Fig. 28**: Musée National d'Art Moderne, Centre Georges Pompidou, Paris, France. Photography by Bertrand Prévost. © CNAC / MNAM / Dist. RMN-Grand Palais / Art Resource, NY. **Fig. 29**: © FLC / ARS, 2015. **Fig. 30**: Art Institute of Chicago; through prior bequest of Marion Livingston and prior gift of Emily Crane Chadbourne, 2006.1. © Sherrie Levine. Courtesy Paula Cooper Gallery, New York. **Fig. 31**: Centro Studi e Archivio della Comunicazione, Parma University, Project Section. **Fig. 32**: Musée National d'Art Moderne, Centre Georges Pompidou, Paris, France. Photography by Georges Meguerditchian. © CNAC / MNAM / Dist. RMN-Grand Palais / Art Resource, NY. **Fig. 33**: Photography by Philippe Ruault. **Fig. 34**: © Pepo Segura—Fundació Mies van der Rohe. **Fig. 35** (1–12, 14): Courtesy of Eisenman Architects. **Fig. 35** (13): Museum of Modern Art, New York; David Childs, Tracy Gardner, Barbara Jakobson, and Jeffrey P. Klein Purchase Funds. Digital image © The Museum of Modern Art / Licensed by SCALA / Art Resource, NY. **Fig. 37**: Concept by Lebbeus Woods, design and construction by architect Paul Anvar. © Estate of Lebbeus Woods.